KATERI TEKAKWITHA

MYSTIC OF THE WILDERNESS

KATERI TEKAKWITHA

MYSTIC OF THE WILDERNESS

MARGARET R. BUNSON

Foreword by
Msgr. Paul A. Lenz

Our Sunday Visitor Publishing Division
Our Sunday Visitor, Inc.
Huntington, Indiana

Foreword

A s a young Catholic high school student, I was aware of the name Kateri Tekakwitha when the saints of the Church were studied, especially the saints of the United States. At that time Mother Frances Cabrini, Mother Elizabeth Ann Seton and Maria Goretti were prominent. I recall, though, the fascination with the Mohawk Indian maiden, Kateri Tekakwitha.

In 1976 I was appointed the sixth director of the Bureau of Catholic Indian Missions, the Church's office established in 1874 to work with the Native American community. I immediately had my memory refreshed with the name of Kateri Tekakwitha as I found a swelling of interest for the advancement of her Cause. She was honored by the Church with the title of *Venerable* in 1943 and people were praying and working to have her named Blessed.

The good news did come in April of 1980 when the Vatican announced Kateri would be declared *Blessed* by Pope John Paul II at a ceremony in St. Peter's Basilica, Vatican City, June 22, 1980. The pleasing news for me was that I was assigned to be in charge of preparations in the United States for the Beatification. When the great day arrived I was selected as one of the fourteen concelebrants of the Mass with the Holy Father, the only one not a member of the hierarchy.

Since the beatification ceremony there has been much activity, especially from and through the Native Americans themselves, and this concern has been supported earnestly by the Church. The interest is far reaching and has fanned out from Auriesville, New York, where she was born, to Caughnawaga, Canada where she died and is buried, to all parts of the North American Continent.

Shortly after the Beatification Ceremony, the Diocese of

Honolulu, Hawaii, where quite a few Native Americans live, noted the Beatification of Kateri with several outstanding events. A commemorative Mass was offered by Bishop John J. Scanlan, then Bishop of Honolulu, a proclamation was signed by the Governor of the State, and other gatherings focused on the life of the first one with Native American blood to be so honored by the Church.

In Hawaii, Maggie Bunson, artist and author, was prominent as the coordinator of the Island celebrations. Always with a keen interest in Church history, she has written this book of new insights on Blessed Kateri, *Kateri Tekakwitha: Mystic of the Wilderness*. One of her books, *Founding of Faith*, relates so well the accounts of Catholics in the American Revolutionary Era. The new book takes one back a step in history and shows the working of the Holy Spirit in the wilderness as the young Kateri was hearing the call of her Creator and was responding.

Blessed Kateri Tekakwitha has been a blessing for the Native American people and everywhere she is held in high regard. Years ago when I served as a missionary in Paraguay, South America a common sight observed in the homes of the people were the pictures of Pope John XXIII and President John Kennedy. Now as I travel to the Indian Reservations and visit the homes, I see many times the photos of Pope John Paul II and Blessed Kateri Tekakwitha.

What Maggie Bunson has done is to let one look behind the wilderness and see this Blessed maiden of the wilderness advance in spirituality, and from that wilderness, have so much influence for her people and for everyone in the world of today.

The book is supportive of the evangelization dreams of the Native American folks. For over three hundred years they heard so often "what the Catholic Church had done for them." Now with great pride, the Native Americans are aware of their evangelization contribution to the Church.

Monsignor Paul A. Lenz
Director
Bureau of Catholic Indian Missions
Washington, D.C.

Introduction

The life of Kateri Tekakwitha is well known in America, but few of us are acquainted with the details of her short existence or with the rich and profound heritage that helped to form her as a vessel of purity. Above all, few Americans realize that the modern Native Americans are a link to a magnificent and vital past on the continent. The Indian nations surviving today are direct descendants of one of the most astounding groups of human beings that ever walked the face of the earth. They are the inheritors of the primitive clans that walked out of Siberia, in the Old World, down the Alaskan and Canadian wilderness, across the American plains, forests and mountains and down to the grassy slopes of Patagonia at the southern tip of the world.

Kateri, herself, was formed by those primitive clans, lived in the wilderness of the Americas, was raised in the traditions of the Iroquois and then emerged as the great flower of purity within the faith. She outdates the American nation by a century, but she endures as a vital link to the past, and as a bridge between the Native American communities of the nation and the Church. She is the Lily of the Mohawks, chosen by God Almighty to be as well the Mystic of the Wilderness. This is her story.

Margaret R. Bunson

Kateri Tekakwitha:
The Lily of the Mohawks

One of the most remarkable figures in the history of the United States is emerging at this time into the mainstream of the American consciousness and is becoming known throughout the entire world. Her image startles modern generations because it whispers of a continental wilderness, of primitive and harrowing eras, and, at the same time, it evokes the spirit of confrontation that took place when the Europeans invaded the North American landscape. Kateri Tekakwitha is the name of this historical figure, and she is called the Lily of the Mohawks. A resident of the tribal lands of the American northeastern territories, she existed long before the colonials decided to forge a new nation in the wilderness. Kateri Tekakwitha was born in 1656 and died in 1680.

What is even more remarkable about Kateri Tekakwitha is the fact that this woman, who died at a very tender age, dwelt in yet another landscape, in the world of the true mystics. She was a contemplative, a soul enraptured by God even in the wilds of a hostile land.

The details of her life have been known to the Native American populations and to Vatican authorities for some time, and she has now received the first honors of the altar, in the process undertaken by Church authorities for canonization. She is known now throughout the world as Blessed Kateri Tekakwitha. *The Positio of the Historical Section of the Sacred Congregation of Rites on the Introduction of the Cause for Beatification and Canonization*

9

and on the Virtues of the Servant of God Katherine Tekakwitha the Lily of the Mohawks, with an introduction dated to 1938, states:

> The servant of God Katherine Tekakwitha was a North American Indian, a genuine redskin, the first of that great and sorely tried human family to be presented to the Sacred Congregation of Rites as a candidate for the honors of the altar.

The opening of the Cause of Kateri, as her name has evolved over the centuries on this continent, was a wondrous event, and many people rejoiced at the appearance of this very special human being as a true symbol of the American past. The words used in describing her origins, however, reflected the thinking of the time and echoed the prevailing ignorance and bias which have taken a toll upon a great people.

Few racial or ethnic groups have suffered the peculiar travesties of justice endured by the various tribes of the Native American people in the United States, a condition which remains unabated in some regions even today. Since the time of the first European intrusion into the Americas, the native populations have been plagued by misconceptions about their origins, their societies, philosophies and even spiritual ideals. Such misconceptions, based on brief encounters, legends or tall tales, and nurtured by indifference or prejudice, have robbed many tribal communities of their lustrous heritage and have reduced their singular accomplishments in the eyes of their fellow citizens.

To begin with, the Native Americans are not Indians, despite the fact that even they refer to themselves as such because of the decades of common use of the term. The Native Americans received the name "Indians" early on, as if they were a band from New Delhi or Calcutta miraculously transported across the Pacific Ocean. The Native Americans have nothing to do with the Indian people of the Asian subcontinent. The name came into use by Europeans after Christopher Columbus arrived in the New World. He was not seeking another exotic continent but a passage to the

East, known then for its spices, silks, jewels and luxury goods. The East had become an almost mythical place because of the tales of Marco Polo and other hardy adventurers who had managed to penetrate its forbidding lands and its secrets.

Columbus believed that he had come to the "Indies," as that part of the world was called in Europe at the time. The name he thus coined for the American territories and for its inhabitants became not only popular but part of the European vocabulary. Until that fateful day 500 years ago, few in Europe had ever contemplated the remote possibility of an entire continent rising out of the ocean between the Old World and the fabled "Indies." Certainly no major European power had ever mounted costly expeditions to America before Columbus stumbled upon it. The fact that he and his co-adventurers discovered the New World while busily seeking another place entirely did not alter the outcome of the event.

The Native Americans, the Indians of the New World, have also been called *redskins* by their fellow countrymen over the centuries as well, as the Vatican document clearly demonstrates even in terms of respect and wonderment. The term *redskin* is so engrained in the American consciousness, in fact, that it has become a vital part of western lore. It is a word that conjures up a myriad of images, of course. No one can imagine a Mountain Man straggling into a fort to warn the settlers with the phrase: "The Native Americans are coming!" *Redskins* served the purpose beautifully, and it has endured. Films, books, television shows and academic studies have used the term over and over again, as the European settlers echoed it in their own time. The truth of the Native American population's coloring has never mattered. Few Americans realize today that Native American groups represent a dazzling variety of hues in their appearance, from very fair to dark brown, much like the newly arrived European population in the beginning of the nation.

The term appears to have come from the French phrase: *peaux rouges*. The early French trappers and hunters who scoured the Canadian and American wilds for furs, encountered the Native Americans or Indians and described them to their companions as *peaux rouges*, setting the basis for the tradition. No actual reason has ever been provided for this particular choice of colors in describing the native populations. One speculates, naturally, that the French came upon the Indians at the end of a long, hot summer, when they were probably reddened or tanned by the sun. This has never been documented, so the mystery remains.

Meanwhile, however, the Europeans of the Old World were beginning to hear of the discovery of such people in the wilderness of America. As tales of their lifestyles, their wars, their arts trickled back to Europe, speculations about their origins became the rage. There was even a suggestion that the Native Americans were actually part of the "lost" tribes of Israel. This idea opened up fervent debates and controversies in Europe's academic and religious circles, but such arguments remained in Europe. The settlers and hunters actually in the New World started to push their way into the untamed continent and had little time to fret over biblical connotations when they met up with the local tribes.

These Europeans were quite single-minded in their intents and purposes. Some came to claim as many fur-bearing animals as possible during each hunting season. Some came to stake out new homesteads and to claim the wilderness as their own. The Mountain Men, the first uniquely American by-products of the wilderness, the hunters and explorers who ranged far and wide over plains and mountains, gained intimate knowledge of the various native communities, for good or for ill. They either became good friends or dreaded enemies of the tribes. Of course, the Mountain Men, individualists who looked down on anyone who needed the trappings of civilization in order to survive, disliked the settlers and the colonists even more than they did the Indians.

The settlers, wanting only the land that belonged to the tribes, hated the Mountain Men and wanted no part in debates about the biblical origins or status of the Native Americans. Entire volumes have been written, in fact, about the process of settling the New World and the ways in which the Indians, despite their original generosity and kindnesses, were rolled back by the relentless tides of immigrants and land grabbers.

Today, despite the common usage of the name *Indian*, the term *Native American* has taken root. This not only demonstrates the fact that everyone else calling himself or herself an American and claiming the United States home, is a newcomer to its shores, but the term *Native American* clearly depicts the centuries of residence which can be verified scientifically for the various tribal groupings.

Originally the ancestors of the Indians were of Mongolian or of some other Asiatic stock. It is known that these ancestors came into the American continent from Siberia some 20,000 years ago, perhaps even earlier. They began their endless treks when *homo sapiens* were evolving and expanding their social skills in the face of a restless, hostile and developing world.

Life in the Siberian tundra, where most of these people originated, was harsh and demanding even in good times. The freezing temperatures, the winds roaring over the marshy plains, the storms that raged over glacier peaks, and the wild animals that roamed the regions threatened all of their progress and even their survival in some areas. Nomadic or semi-nomadic in their lifestyles, these groups were linked to the seasonal changes of the earth and to the migrations of the various game animals. These were human beings involved in the last stages of what is called the Great Ice Age; a period of violent upheavals and dangerous landscapes, as the earth itself was in the process of change.

In the fourth and final movements of the polar ice formations, called the Wisconsin Glaciation (in Europe designated as the Wurm Glaciation), the entire northern hemisphere of the earth was locked in the embrace of giant glaciers. These vast mounds of ice and snow, as deep as fifty feet in some areas, crept steadily southward, leveling small peaks, ripping apart forests and glades and sending boulders crashing into frozen wastes. All of the land features known today were invisible as the original formations were erased by the glaciers moving inch by inch to the American Great Lakes. Everything in the path of such massive mountains of snow and ice was molded into a barren wasteland; frozen and gutted by the cold and by the pressures of the weight. In turn, the sea levels at the time were probably from 200 to 400 feet lower than they are today.

Between Alaska of the New World and Siberia of the Old, now separated by the Bering Straits, there was a land mass, believed by some to have been approximately 1,000 miles wide. This land mass, now called Beringia, served as a bridge between the two continents — rising and falling, settling and thickening as the glaciers inched forward on their southern journeys or suffered changes in the warming winds. Beringia was probably not much more than a water-soaked plain most of the time, a favorite haunt for migrating herds and smaller types of game, including those animals that preyed on the great masses of others moving across the horizons. These herds were the lure for the ancestors of the Indians, bringing them onto the frozen meadows and marshes of Beringia to seek their food. As the herds wandered far afield, entering the American continent, the hunting tribes followed. Behind them their clans and their families straggled along, entering a new world which beckoned through the mists and the snows.

These human beings certainly did not set out with any clear notion of claiming a new continent for their own kind. They had no idea that they were about to settle a New World. These were primitive people, carrying simple weapons, hunting and gathering in the wake of the migrating herds and stopping only for campfires and rest when the herds appeared to have settled or when their meager stocks were sufficient to tide them over such respites.

They wore pelts and skins, and they ate what they could find, using basic tools and utensils. Certainly they lacked any cosmic awareness about the destiny of mankind as a whole or their own clans in particular. If they fretted or discussed matters they related to the next day's march, the need for food and rest, and the care of the fires, which would have been considered as sacred.

Beringia would have appeared as just another stretch of land opening before them as they moved ever onward in search of meat and skins. The idea of a continental bridge was far beyond them. It would not have come within the scope of their reasoning at all. In time, of course, that bridge collapsed, washed away with the great chunks of ice that were entering the sea as the glaciers withdrew and gave birth to the straits. With their only avenue of retreat behind them, if they even thought of such a retreat, the groups were forced to remain on the American continent. It is probable that these tribes made no attempt to retrace their steps at all, as one territory in that climate looked like another. The earth, however, was giving way to warming trends, and the ice and the freezing temperatures were becoming seasonal. As the clans trekked southward, seeking sheltering caves and passageways through the remaining ice fields, they followed the herds which sought their own fresh domains.

It is believed that these first Native Americans followed the Brooks Range through the Mackenzie River Valley or wandered south through the Yukon. Their far-ranging journeys are astounding, considering the fact that they crossed the U.S. territories, with many reaching South America and the Andes in time. The great cultures that arose in the regions of Mesoamerica and in the realms of Peru are testaments to the travels made in primitive conditions by vulnerable human beings, following paths on foot.

Sites from the historical Paleo-Indian Period, divided into Early and Late (c. 15,000 - 8,000 B.C.) are being uncovered all across North America today. These range from Onion Portage, Alaska, to Tepexpan, Mexico (where remains of true mammoth hunters have been discovered), and from Laguna Beach, California, to Plenge, New Jersey. Such sites demonstrate the great flexibility of these first migrants who staked out their own lands and then adapted to the demands of the local environments. Distinct ages of evolutional development can be documented in the remains of these places, determined by the presence of stone weapon points, such as the Clovis, Folsom and Plano. Each new era represented changes and improved skills as the people discovered methods of insuring their survival and ways of pooling their resources for the benefit of all.

The migrants moved steadily across North America as others trekked southward. Each region, now called micro-environments, offered them a variety of fruits, nuts, small animals, fish, birds, herbs and grasses. They learned to band together to hunt the larger game, as they became skilled at fortifying their settlements against attacks by wild animals. These creatures were immense and ferocious, and there was a great diversity of such animals in this period, including what is called mega-fauna, or large game. The three-ton woolly mammoth roamed the plains, alongside the American mastadon, the giant sloth, the American lion, and camelids, whose surviving descendants are still in South America in the form of llamas, guanacos and vicunas. The Dire Wolves, believed by some scholars to have stood six feet at the shoulders, bears, tapirs, saber-toothed tigers, the great bison, giant beavers, some weighing as much as 300 pounds, roamed the hills and plains along with peccaries.

As the tribes extended their hunting ranges and began new experiments with lifestyles that were adapted to the seasons and to the newly found environments, changes took place within their ranks. Some groups perished because they could not manage the challenges and horizons that loomed before them at every turn of the trail. Others were incorporated into the larger, more self-sufficient groups that emerged in large homelands. New weapons appeared, new ways of defending themselves against animals or of stalking them as prey, and a social order was developed as were their skills. The Native Americans were at home in the New World, where they would hone their spiritual and religious concepts —

especially those of a cosmogonic nature, those that explained the universe and the role of human beings. These Indians asked themselves the primordial questions that have haunted humanity since the beginning of time: They asked about their origins, their sojourns upon the earth, and about their ultimate destiny beyond the grave. At the same time, they became one with nature and with the seasons, forming their unique sense of the earth and its moods, of the land, the sky and the elements. With this relationship came a definite concept of stewardship, of care and concern for all living things.

The sprawling, endless North American wilderness serves as one of four distinct and powerful landscapes in the life of Kateri Tekakwitha. These landscapes, each one having its own impetus and spurs, were destined to converge in her personality and in her faith. At the same time, they blended and then contradicted one another as she made her way to her own mystical end.

The American wilderness was the oldest and the most basic of the landscapes in Kateri's existence, because it was a force that not only shaped the native groups residing there but altered the outlook of the Europeans who crowded on its shore. At the close of the historical Archaic Period, around 300 B.C., the American continent was home to many tribal communities, each one developing the unique characteristics that would mark their presence in the forests and plains. The various geographical locations enforced the differing lifestyles on the tribes, and warfare among them also led them into expansions or migrations to even more distant wild lands.

In the southwest, for example, the startling sophistication of the ruins of the Anasazi clearly demonstrate the fact that they recognized a need for strategic defenses early on. The mounds of Adena, the Hopewell culture and others in the Midwest depict a well formed death cult, as well as a confederated government that could wield vast human resources alongside colonization policies. Monks Mound, in Missouri, for instance, was 100 feet high, almost as tall as the Great Pyramid of Giza, in Egypt. The site of that mound is believed to have been the abode of as many as 30,000 to 40,000 American Indians.

The desert nomadic tribes followed their flocks in other areas, and farms emerged in the southwest, linked by trade with the towering civilizations of Mesoamerica, the Aztecs and others. These trade routes, expanding farms, mounds, and the trapping sites in the forests blended into the first homelands. There mountains crested the sky, the seasons danced through the years, and the earth and the stars revolved in an endless universe of order and faith.

In the northeastern part of America, Kateri's own region, at the close of the Archaic Period, around 300 B.C., vast forests and woodlands covered the area. Oaks, hickories, chestnuts and other trees formed beautiful expanses of thick foliage, interspersed by glades, rivers, lakes and plains. Within these woods a rich variety of plants and animals flourished, drawing communities of early tribes to their rich resources and natural havens.

Many indications of early habitation have been documented in this part of the United States, including ceramics and signs of an evolving burial ritual system that used cremation. Such a burial system indicates a growing religious sense — the asking of the primordial questions — and the awareness of the spiritual side of human existence. The Forest People of North America, as the early inhabitants of the northeastern sections are now referred to as, used all of the natural resources displayed before them in their chosen lands. The trees of the forest, for example, provided the raw materials for the walls of their residences, the bark especially, and the trees were used as well for spears, arrows, trays, canoes, stakes, litters, nets and snowshoes. Within the forests there were nuts, fruits, wild fowls, rabbits, woodchucks, beaver, moose, elk, caribou, deer, antelope, sheep and bears, who assumed — along with the eagle — positions of ceremonial powers and deep religious significances.

The Forest People used the wigwam, which was erected by taking four saplings and bending them toward the center as a framework. Tree bark was then stretched and fastened into place as walls. The interior of the wigwam was covered with swamp grass and fir branches. This then was covered with moose hides and used as sleeping pallets. Other pelts were used as rugs, or as bits of ornamentation, including those of the North American wolf, coyote, fox, wolverine, rabbit, raccoon, weasel, skunk, gopher, marmot, squirrel, chipmunk, marten, beaver, ermine, mink, and even mice.

The wigwam differed from the teepee depicted in the historical photographs and paintings of the Plains People. The teepee, or *tipi*, was made with three or four main poles, supported by twenty to twenty-four lesser poles, and standing as high as 20 feet, being 30 feet across. The teepee was collapsible and could be moved as the nomadic migrations with the herds began.

The Forest People, Kateri's clans, did not wander about but used hunters, called the Woodland Warriors, to keep the larders stocked. These Woodland Warriors were solitary, patient and enduring, bound to the earth in a unique and very real fashion. They had a particular sensitivity to the landscapes of their regions, and they understood even the most subtle changes in sounds and movements about them. The forests, the plains and the river banks alerted them to dangers, assured them when all was clear, and even signaled the coming of a new season. Birds and animals manifested alarm when strangers were in the victinity. The plants, birds and animals also underwent changes when winter was approaching rapidly on the land. The spring melt was evident, as the coming of the hot, dry winds of summers.

By becoming one with the animals and plants of the forests, the Woodland Warriors used every sense to track and locate game, to protect themselves from peril and to scout against enemy raiding parties that could endanger their villages. Each one of them was trained to serve as a truly superior person, one who understood his or her unique place in the overall scheme of nature. Some women in the tribes proved themselves skilled in these capacities and were so honored. Alongside the men they preserved the land and its resources, showed concern for the environment and a sense of oneness with the woodlands that served them so faithfully.

By A.D. 500, the bow and the arrow had been invented, used alongside spears and lances with flint tips. Each tribe had from five to ten principal hunters. The bows used by these Woodland Warriors were made from the ash, yew or mulberry tree, bent into shape over hot ashes. Some had bone inlays or sinew, and twisted fibers strengthened the ends or the middle of the bow.

Arrows were designed in individual styles, easily recognized by other tribes (and later by the settlers). The feathers of eagles, buzzards, turkeys or hawks normally decorated these arrows. Great hunters could shoot targets some fifty yards away, and they could continue rapid-fire volleys, pulling the arrows from their quivers and shooting on and on against enemies. Some tribes, including the Iroquois, are reported as well to have used eight-foot blowguns, with poisoned darts, feathered with thistledown, and powered by the lungs of the user.

The Forest People carried fire from one camp to another when moving on to seasonal sites. Such moves were normally dependent upon changing weather conditions and the signs of coming freezes, as the tribes sought more sheltered havens for the harsh winter months. Fields were cultivated in certain seasons of the year, with flint corn being planted in May and harvested in June. Squash, beans, pumpkins, gourds, sweet potatoes, manioc, tomatoes, nuts and a form of tobacco (*Nicotiana rustica*) were also part of the crops either cultivated or regularly gathered.

Most of the Woodland People wore skins, beautifully cleaned and prepared, fashioned into leggings and shirts or into blouses and skirts. Loin cloths were made out of deerskins, and mantles were used in colder months. These articles of clothing were decorated with quills, eagle feathers, shells, and beads, and jewelry was popular, especially items which were made out of stone and copper.

The actual world of the Iroquois, one of the major Forest People groups, and an astonishingly sophisticated group in a political and social sense, forms the second landscape of Kateri's life on earth. It was formulated by the first landscape, the rugged American wilderness, but it was a highly complex and energetic environment which took into consideration the needs of the weak and the infirm as well as those who could make constant contributions.

The Iroquois were called by that name by the French because they supposedly ended most of their sentences with the word *hiro*, which means, "I have spoken," and *koue*, which is the sound of a small cry, probably made for emphasis. The tribe called itself the *Hodensaunee*, "the people of the Longhouses." Historians have honored the Iroquois with the title: "The Romans of the New World" because of their governmental systems and their intelligent, reasoning concept of citizen participation on all levels. The enemies of the Iroquois called them the "Kinsmen of the Wolves." This was an honorable title, one given with respect, and it was due to the relentless ferocity of the Iroquois when attacked. They spoke their own language, which was related to the Algonquin and the Macro-Siouan tongues.

By the time the first European settlers entered the American wilderness and the domain of the Iroquois, which was quite vast, the various groups which constituted the entire Nation were settled in their homelands, which they guarded fiercely. The Iroquois were comfortable in their deciduous birch, beech, maple and elm forests, which gave way to firs and spruce in the higher elevations. The Iroquois territory consisted of the land south of Lake Ontario, in a region dotted by streams, valleys and hills. The lovely Finger Lakes were in their domain, and there the Mohawk River flowed into the graceful Appalachian Mountains. In eastern Iroquoia, as the first Canadians named the area, there were vast stands of oak, chestnuts, and poplars, broken by the valleys of the Hudson River tributaries. It was a region of unending horizons, beautiful, crystal clear waters and natural resources that had been carefully husbanded over the decades.

It is believed that the Iroquois migrated from the regions north of the St. Lawrence River, although there are some rather remarkable references to them in the records of the Pawnees, which would place their origins far beyond the Mississippi River. It is now accepted by many scholars that the original inhabitants of the region claimed in time by the Iroquois were the Owascas, a farming people who raised corn crops as early as A.D. 1300 on many sites.

The Iroquois were also farmers, despite their fame as Woodland Warriors. They used the *swidden* or slash-and-burn techniques for preparing land for crops and harvests. They cut down stands of trees in order to claim new fields, setting fire to the remaining trunks, and the flames devoured the low lying shrubs in the same plots. The resulting ashes were used as fertilizer for the claimed land in return. Each new field prepared by the slash-and-burn technique was then tilled until it became barren. It was then abandoned, and the farmers moved on to the next area. Relying chiefly on farming for sustenance could then result in wholesale devastation of vast tracts of land as is seen in the southern regions of the continent.

The Iroquois were perhaps saved from land decimation by the fact that they relied more upon hunting and gathering than on cultivation of crops. Consequently, the land's resources were not as quickly taxed. It has been estimated that each community used as many as 2,000 deer each season. The animal was eaten, but clothing, weapons and utensils were then manufactured out of its carcass. The crops that were grown by the Iroquois included three that they revered as bountiful nurturers of life. They called these the "Three Sisters," and they were corn, squash and beans generally. Such crops could be stored away for the lean months of winter, and they were lush and beautiful in the fields. Tobacco was another prized crop, grown for ceremonial uses, as the idea of smoke rising into the heavens was viewed as a salute to the Great Spirit and his heavenly companions.

In this second landscape of Kateri's life, bound to the American wilderness, the first landscape, the people of Iroquoia, which is roughly modern New York State, had formed a complex confederation of several tribes around the fourteenth century A.D. The Five Nations Confederacy, the *Ho-dé-no-sau-nee*, the People of the Longhouses, was composed of the following tribes:

- Mohawks — the *Ga-né-a-ga-o-no* — the Flint Possessing People;
- Oneidas — the *O-na-yoté-ka* — the People of the Stone;
- Onondagas — the *O-nun-da-ga-o-no* — the People on the Hills;
- Cayugas — the *Gue-u-gweh-o-no* — the People at the Mucky Lands (marshes);
- Senecas — the *Nun-da-wa-o-ne* — the Great Hill People.

In time the Tuscaroras joined the federation as well, but in the beginning the lands held in common were divided into five strips, running from north to south, ranging from the Hudson River to the shores of Lake Erie. Each tribe had its own lake or river system, and the region abounded in forests, hills and natural resources. Such land divisions were called the "Longhouse" (hence the name chosen by the tribes for the confederacy), and they averaged 200 miles apiece.

Within each Longhouse the tribes maintained their own councils and their own ceremonial fires, which were symbols of authority, reason and justice. The eastern door of the Five Nations, Iroquoia, was guarded by the Longhouse of the Mohawks, the people of Kateri Tekakwitha.

The Five Nations came into being because of a vision of a holy man named Dekanawidah (or Tekanawita), who dreamed in 1570 of a region shared in common by former competitive tribes. This remarkable sage envisioned the Five Nations joined under the Tree of Great Peace, *Kaianerekowa*, bonded in brotherhood, mutual respect and in the desire to protect the integrity and rights of each individual man and woman within its borders. Dekanawidah confided his dream to a Mohawk warrior named Hiawatha, and together they prepared a message for all of the other tribes in the area.

Hiawatha then began to visit the villages of the tribes, speaking to the chiefs and the people before their camp fires. He related how Dekanawidah had been given this great vision, which was a gift to the people from the Great Spirit. Oratory was one of the exquisite talents of the Iroquois, and with an image of the sacred tree, peace, and the tribes living as one against all enemies, came resolve. The elders and the tribal councils agreed to unite the people for the common good of all.

It was decided that each tribe would remain its own entity, nurturing the traditions and ideals that had been forged over the centuries in the American wilderness. Each one of these groups had their own views of the earth and the roles of men and women, but they shared in common the concept of the "hearth" family, which consisted of a man and his wife and their offspring. These were related, in turn, to the members of the same matriarchal lineage — the family traced through the mother's heirs — and then to the clan. The clans of the various nations had specific designations and duties. These included the clans of the Turtle, Painted Turtle, the Great Name Bearers, the Ancient Name Bearers, the Great Bear, the Ancient Bear, the Large Snipe (or Plover), the Small Snipe (or Plover), the Hawk, the Deer, the Standing Rock, etc. Each clan formed the tribe, which formed the nation.

The Senecas are reported as being the last to consent to the union, but eventually they saw the advantages of being part of a unique social experiment in a wild and sometimes hostile world. Not only would the natural resources be shared and protected, but each nation could count on a unified and sophisticated military force. It has been estimated that the total Iroquois population at the time of Kateri Tekakwitha was approximately 25,000. Such a population could put 3,000 men into the field easily, and they were well trained warriors, working in a highly developed military fashion against their enemies. Warfare in the region had taken a grim toll over the decades, and the Iroquois were determined to protect their domain. When the Senecas consented to the Five Nations Confederacy, it was said that the members clasped hands "so firmly that a falling tree could not sever them." So stable and profitable did the organization prove, in fact, that within a half century the Five Nations were the most powerful Native Americans on the North American continent.

A Great Council, composed of representatives of all of the united tribes, elected by the women matriarchs, met at Onondaga, under the Tree of Great Peace, the mighty symbol which was such an integral part of Dekanawidah's vision. An eagle did perch high on that mighty tree according to traditional rememberings, keeping watch over the Council. This confederation of representatives was called the Council of the Fifty Sachems, although after the initial gathering only forty nine were ever present. The placed designated for Hiawatha remained empty for all time after his passing, in memory of his courageous journey to bring union to the people. The Sachems had to be chosen with specific virtues in mind. They had to be honest men, able to remain above petty village or clan politics. Their symbol of office was the antlers of the deer, and during their ceremonies of installation, the people gathered to witness their acceptance of the offices. A Conferring of Rank festival followed, with the new Sachem catering the entire affair.

The Great Council Fire burned whenever the Sachems were in session, and the smoke of that fire was a symbol far and wide that men of reason and good will had met to speak words of wisdom and justice. Such meetings were prolonged and filled with elegant oratory, and each one was opened by prayers of thanksgiving for the earth and all of the natural resources, as bestowed upon mankind by the Great Creator, called the source and ruler of health and of life. In this manner the Council served as an extension of the Iroquois families and clans, and the members provided solutions for many of the problems that came to the tribes over the generations.

This was not a general court, however, and it was not available to the average Indian. Not everyone could walk up and address the Sachems freely. If a problem arose, such as a quarrel over property or rights, an individual had to discuss the matter first with his own family members, then with the clan elders, and then with the chiefs of the entire nation. Smaller issues were normally settled within one of those circles, and there was no need to bring it before the assembled representatives. Wars, trade affairs, contacts with Europeans or threats from outsiders were part of the Great Council's discussions because they involved the entire Five Nations or led to events that would eventually concern everyone.

Alongside this Great Council were the Keepers of Faith and other elders chosen to maintain the moral attitudes and the traditions of the people. Both men and women served in this capacity. The women were also the undisputed leaders of the various villages and residences. Most of these villages were approximately two acres wide, fortified by log palisades with towers and platforms for defense against attacks. Such fortifications were erected on hilltops or on rises, set back from streams so that they would not be vulnerable to floods or to the war canoes of raiding enemies. The clans living within each town had their own longhouses, which were some 400 feet long and 22 feet wide.

Such residences were constructed with sapling frames, which were tied to form a rounded top, with large pieces of elm bark on the sides, serving as walls. Smoke holes were formed in the roof, and there were hearths built into the floors. A central corridor was fashioned by placing two rows of posts the length of the house, which marked off the partitions for individual families. Inside there were cooking hearths, utensils, beds, and general living areas. Outside, the family kept corn cribs, storehouses and smoke racks for game. Pottery and clay pipes were fashioned by the women in each village, some having small faces on them, a religious symbol. The pottery was distinguished normally by high rims. The small faces reflected the prominence of the False Face Society, a group that performed during certain festivals and were believed to possess great magical powers, including the ability to lure beneficial spirits out of the forest to cure the sick and the ailing.

The Mohawks, Kateri's people, are believed to have numbered around 5,000 at the time of her birth, and they had several major towns, each ruled by three chiefs who worked together for the common good. The oldest woman of each village was the matriarch, who governed all activities to the edge of the forest, where her authority ended. The Warriors of the Woodlands, the males, dominated there.

The idea of having women in control was based on the creation traditions, called cosmogony, of the Iroquois people. The Mohawks and their fellow confederation members explained how the earth, the sky and humans were fashioned by narrating a story about Sky-Woman, a female spirit, who was pushed out of heaven. She landed on an island far below, a site created by a muskrat that brought mud from under the sea and piled it in mounds on the shell of a giant turtle. As the turtle grew, so did the island. Sky Woman lived there alone. She had been impregnated by the Earth Holder, another powerful spirit, and she gave birth to a daughter in her exile. This daughter, in turn, was magically impregnated and bore two sons: the Great Spirit (*Tharoniawagon* or *Ha-wen-ne-yu*) and the Evil Spirit (*Ha-ne-go-ate-geh*, the Evil-Minded). In giving birth to this last child, the daughter died.

The Great Spirit then fashioned the sun from his mother's head and made the moon and stars out of her body. He fashioned the rivers, the seas and the mountains and then made man, plants and animals. This creation story, linked to the role of the female, provided the Iroquois with their sense of oneness with nature and all living things. During all of this creativity, of course, the Evil

Spirit summoned up the vices of anger, war, envy as well as other sins and dangerous creatures that could threaten the humans fashioned by his brother. Eventually the two spirits fought one another, and they engaged in a battle which raged for two entire days. The Evil-Minded was forced to flee to the underworld, as the Great Spirit proved victorious. The evil of the fallen one, however, remained on earth, as did the dangerous creatures that he had brought into the world. There were also lesser spirits who worked in the service of the Great Spirit when order was restored. These were beings such as the Thunderer, the spirit of lightning and storms, and Ga-oh, the spirit of the wind.

Many festivals and ceremonies honored the Great Spirit and the various seasons of the year, and the villages participated in activities of the year with enthusiasm, sometimes sharing a festival, sometimes honoring ideals or spirits that were unique to their own traditions. The tribes also shared in wars, an aspect of Iroquois life that remained constant despite the united military efforts and the expertise which they showed in battle. Neighboring tribes many times attacked the Five Nations in order to gain territories, and such groups were repulsed after campaigns. The Iroquois also initiated some of these assaults, and when they were victorious they were merciless against the fallen enemies. In time, of course, the Europeans would become their major enemy, sometimes linked with traditionally hostile tribes. War was never taken lightly by the Five Nations because it involved military forces from all of the members and endangered the villages. Once started, however, such a war was carried on until victory, at which time the Iroquois conducted wholescale reigns of terror on the foes, prompted by the desire to make their powers known enough to discourage other groups from making costly errors.

The Iroquois carried shields into battle, made of wood, and the warriors used tomahawks, an Algonquin word for wooden war club. An axe blade was attached to the stem of the tomahawks. Breastplates were also worn, made out of reeds and quite capable of deflecting arrows and lances. The warriors used bows and arrows, lances and spears in hand-to-hand combat.

The French, who encountered the Iroquois in battle, said that they "approach like foxes, fight like lions and disappear like birds." Part of the war ritual — in a tradition that dates back to early times — was the famous *coup*, the French term for the Indian custom of daring. Warriors tried to reach a well-defended enemy, creeping into camps to touch a foe, to mark him or to slay him in the circle of his own allies. Sometimes the mark was enough to rank as *coup*, but often the Iroquois managed to slay their enemies in this fashion. Skill and stealth were necessary in this type of assault, and those who counted *coup* among their activities were honored by friends and enemies alike. This was all part of the Iroquois reputation for bravery, ferocity and intelligence.

Victorious in battle most of the time, at least until the Europeans brought sophisticated weapons to bear, along with vastly over-whelming numbers, the Iroquois were not compassionate to captives. Anyone falling into their hands was tied with leather thongs and marched back to the Iroquois village or outpost, normally beaten along the way. At the village, the women elders decided the fate of each captive. Some were chosen as slaves and some condemned to die in a hideous fashion. The women, even the small girls, tortured prisoners, and the torment was designed to last for days on end. The Mohawks honored the war god Agreskoue (or A-gris-ko-ue), and captives died as his tribute, which was why their deaths were prolonged and filled with as much pain as possible.

On the whole, despite the wars and the torture, the Iroquois society worked well as a structure designed to provide each individual member with a specific role. Everyone worked for the good of the whole. Each man, woman and child also knew his or her place and was well provided for by an extended family.

Vigilance was their strong point always, especially among the Mohawks, whose lands guarded the eastern gateway to the Five

Nations. The Mohawks had been given the lands from the Hudson River through Lake George, Lake Champlain and the Richelieu River. They had major villages on the banks of the Mohawk River, including Gandaouage (Ossernenon), Gandagoron and Tionntoquen.

The Europeans entering the Mohawk domain found themselves face to face with a compact, highly efficient and sophisticated people. The French composed the bulk of the invaders in the early periods. These started entering the Mohawk lands as trappers and hunters at first. Then they arrived as the allies of the Hurons and the Algonquins, the hated and traditional enemies of the Iroquois.

The Europeans formed the third landscape of Blessed Kateri's life. The crude and vivacious trappers were part of the French entourage, but they were only the vanguard. Behind them came the French priests, Jesuits mostly, and behind them came the French armies. The French priests would prove diligent, courageous and daring in their desire to bring Christ and the Church to the nations in the American wilderness, and in time they would offer not only a physical refuge but a marvelous recognition of Kateri's unique role and her many gifts of grace.

Within the gentle mantle of understanding and respect offered her by the priests, Kateri entered the last and the ultimate landscape of her life. She became one with the mystical realm in which she burned with contemplation, the union of the soul with God. This is stark domain for the unworthy or the unprepared. For those who had been granted the mystical graces, however, it was a place of inestimable joy. Kateri understood the basic tenet of human life, the simple truth that such a sojourn upon the earth is short and only a bridge into eternity. She understood as well that a human life should be spent not in gathering material goods or honors but in devotion, in the act of giving praise and thanks to Almighty God. Her own Mohawk background provided a framework for understanding that each man and woman on the earth is not alone or special but part of a whole; a single unit in the unending creation of the Father, who is the source of life and health, especially within the soul.

Now it is sometimes difficult for modern believers to think of a Native American in the wilderness of the New World, the product of a tribe of the forest, becoming a great mystic. Kateri lived 100 years before the United States was conceived, and she was from a people whose very life-style contradicted the ideals of the European-centered Catholic faith. For this reason especially her mystical gifts, her role in the spirit, demonstrate the great mystery of God's choosing of the human soul for his own designs.

All humans can pray and gain graces, living as good Christians and trying to put into their daily routines the commandments of Jesus. The mystic, however, is led on a different path, one not always recognized or understood by the average person. Some call the mystic's path the "Dark Way," the "Way of Shadows," the "Way of Divine Love." It is not open to anyone not chosen by God alone.

Kateri, orphaned, half blind, scarred by illness and of little worth in her own world, was destined for a greatness of the spirit that spans the centuries and reflects the landscapes in which she existed for so brief a time. These landscapes would collide, confound and torment, eventually robbing her of life, but they would also mold one of the most remarkable, hidden human beings to ever walk the trails of early America. She has been called the Lily of the Mohawks, but perhaps another title should be given to her as well: "Mystic of the Wilderness."

Kateri Tekakwitha was born in 1656 at Ossernenon, the Mohawk fortress called Gandaouague, near modern Auriesville in New York. Her name was originally Tekakwitha, or Tegarouite (translated by some scholars as meaning she who puts things in order), or as Tegahkouita (translated as meaning one who advances or cuts the way before her). The name was not chosen by her parents probably as anything of a prophetic nature, but it does have some rather interesting connotations from a historical viewpoint and has been the subject of some scholarly debate. The addition of Kateri, or Katherine, the name which she now bears within honor before the altars of the universal Church, was the result of her conversion and baptism.

Her father was a Mohawk chief of some prominence, belonging to the Tortoise clan of the nation, one of the designated groups listed by the Great Council at the beginning of the Five Nations Confederacy. The tortoise, along with other animals and birds, as well as ancestors, served as symbols of virtue, of powers and special relationships to the spirit world. Some scholars give his name as Kenhoronkwa, and they list him as the war chief of the village and the clan.

Kateri's mother is listed by scholars as an Algonquin woman, named Kahenta. She was captured during a Mohawk raid on her people, probably in the assault recorded at Three Rivers. Judged worthy of slavery by the women elders of Gandaouague when she was brought into the village, she worked among the Mohawks, fulfilling commands and performing the usual feminine chores. In time, however, Kenhoronkwa, took notice of her, and he married her, giving her full rights in the Mohawk nation. This adoption policy was not common, as the Mohawks did not have to wed a woman captive in order to use them as mates. The Five Nations Confederacy, however, allowed for the legal adoption of alien people, and the chief took advantage of the ruling.

Kahenta was a Christian, having been baptized and trained at the Catholic mission in Quebec. This would have been an additional stigma for her to bear if she had not displayed all of the Christian virtues. As a modest and gentle Christian, she was certainly different from the other maidens of the Mohawk village. She showed kindness and tolerance whenever she went among her captors, accepting ill treatment without complaints and showing a basic good will about her condition. As the other young women liked fine clothes, jewelry and flirtatious relationships, Kahenta would have appeared ideal for a war chief who perhaps hoped to become one of the Great Sachems in time.

There were Jesuits in the area at the time, but Kahenta probably did not see any of them. She would not have gone to their Church without her husband's permission, and he would not have offered it. As the war chief he was aware of the political and military situation facing the Mohawks. The French, along with the Hurons, Algonquins and Mohicans, were the enemies of the Five Nations. The presence of the Jesuits did not console the chief or his contemporaries, perhaps reminding them of the martyrdom of other Jesuits on the same site years before. Eventually the Jesuits at Ossernenon were warned by their Christian converts and admirers that a plot was being formed to slay them. The priests left the village in 1658.

It should be remembered that the Mohawks and other nations of the Iroquois had good reason to dislike the Europeans. The French, Dutch and English were moving into their lands and siding with their tribal enemies. The Jesuits, despite their unique purpose, their dedication and their love of the people, represented the presence of the white men to the Native Americans. They preached to the people about the Prince of Peace, but their counterparts were attacking villages and usurping the natural resources of the land.

At the same time, the Iroquois had developed a profound religious system of their own, one that was based on centuries of tradition, from the time of the great migration into the New World. They had spiritual concepts of their own making, and an awareness of their place in nature. Many of the older Iroquois, perhaps even Kenhoronkwa, must have felt a certain outrage when they heard the missionary sermons. They must have wanted to delay the inevitable collapse of their world by ridding themselves and their village of the Blackrobes, as the Jesuits were called by the Native Americans. The plot and its warnings drove the priests from the village, and the Mohawks stayed grim and alert, poised to fight against the French especially, even as other tribes within the Confederation pondered the wisdom of making peace with the white men and their armies.

Kateri would have been carried on her mother's back, wrapped in an elaborately decorated papoose, as Kahenta joined the other women in gathering wood, berries, nuts and fruits. They pounded corn, brought drinking water from the nearby crystal clear stream, and hunted down the hives of bees for precious honey. Corn, squash and beans, the Three Sisters, the Nurturers, were raised in farming plots, along with tobacco. The women tended these plots, and they used the products along with the carcasses brought in by the Woodland Warriors for food, clothing, weapons, utensils and other decorative items.

Village life was exciting, even when the men were not preparing for war and singing their chants which promised death to the enemies of the nation. Deeply religious, the people celebrated elaborate festivals throughout the year, very much in accordance with the seasonal changes and honoring the various resources which came to them as a result of the earth's bounty in different times of the year. Like their ancestors who had trekked across the Bering Straits, these people were at the mercy of nature and its crops. They understood that they lived as tenants on the land, always storing up against the lean, cold times when the snow would mantle the forests and fields with a crippling whiteness. The animals hid in their lairs, and the birds fled the freezing wilderness for warmer climates in the south. Even the nuts and berries fell victim to freezing rains and winds, as the earth shuddered and settled down for months of cold and wet.

The festivals held throughout the Iroquois lands, like those of other Native American communities, were thus related to the natural cycles as they saw them reflected in the earth and in the seasons. Some of the celebrations were listed in the documents of the Five Nations Confederacy, seen as religious and reverential traditions that would unite new generations and bind the entire Iroquois people to the past. These festivals were intended not only as a demonstration of the Indians' gratitude to the Great Spirit but also as events that would provide a break in the day to day schedules, coming as diversions, as grand occasions which brought out the creative skills of the people as well as their good spirits and their sense of unity.

The first festival of the spring was called Thanks to the Maple, or *O-ta-de-none'-ne-o Na Wa'ta*. In most villages it was simply referred to as The Maple Dance. It was a feast celebrating the precious sweet sap offered by the maple trees of the vicinity each year, a sweetener that was used in diverse ways by the Iroquois women and relished by one and all. The Iroquois did use honey, but they particularly liked the flavor of maple syrup. The feast honoring the maple lasted only one day but was preceded by some rather remarkable ceremonies. The Keepers of the Faith, those elders that were given charge of the morals and the religious aspects of the participating nations, announced the coming of the festival when the sap started to flow in the maple trees of the woodlands. The celebration was always preceded by a general confession of sins or wrongdoing by the people.

This "Meeting for Repentance," as it was called, was an integral part of almost every celebration held within Iroquoia. A wampum belt, the beaded piece of material that served as a symbol of religious power, as a message during negotiations, or as an insignia of worth, was used during this "Meeting For Repentance." In this case the wampum beads were all white, signifying the special purpose of the belt. The Iroquois believed that anything pure white in animals was a sign of the Great Spirit's own partiality. One by one, holding the wampum belt, the men, women and children of the villages admitted all of the things that they had done wrong over the past months. They all promised reformation of character and better conduct in the future, not only for their own sakes but for the good of the entire nation. This is an extraordinary social custom, particularly in the wilderness of the Americas. Such an admittance clearly demonstrates that the Iroquois were a deeply moral people, at least according to their own religious and spiritual evolution, and they were a people quite conscious of the role of the individual in the well-being of the whole. In many cases the "Meeting for Repentance" was held in a central location, attended by the people of the surrounding towns.

A great feast was also prepared for the occasion by the village matrons, although it appears that the Iroquois did not hold large banquets, with everyone gathered together. The women of the various clans and families simply gathered up the food for their own relatives and kinsmen and took it to the village or to some distant site, where they ate it in private celebrations.

As with most occasions, speakers addressed the assembled, speaking of the traditional duties of the individual, according to his or her rank and state in the community. Always the people were told about the need to act in common, to live in harmony, avoiding gossip, envy and scandal. Orphans, the aged and the ill were singled out by these speakers, as they had been by the founders of the Five Nations, as individuals worthy of special care and concern. The Great Spirit, everyone was told, watched the good acts of men and rewarded them, especially if the acts were carried out in his name. These sermons were followed by dances, another form of religious experience, and then by games and athletic contests.

When the planting season arrived in Iroquoia, the villages celebrated the Planting Feast, the *A-yent-wa-ta*. This was similar in most respects to the Maple Dance. During the summer, if the weather was hot and dry, the people held festivals honoring *He' no*, the Thunderer, at which time the elders begged for rain for the parched earth. Again the Iroquois recognized the fact that they were vulnerable to the elements and to the processes of nature which could be quite oblivious to the needs of humans in any given region. The lack of rain was most often viewed as a punishment for some unknown crime by one of the members of the tribe, and the celebration was staged in order to appease the spirit of the rain.

The *Ha-nun-da-' yo*, the Strawberry Festival, was held in honor of this tasty fruit of the year. Similar to the previous festivals, this one was unique in that strawberries were gathered and cooked with maple syrup, forming a deliciously sweet jelly-like substance, which was distributed to everyone attending the festival. The whortleberry, another favored fruit, was greeted by the same type of festival in some regions.

The *Ah-dake'-wa-o*, or the Festival of the Green Corn, continued for four days, as this crop was of particular importance to the Five Nations, as it was vital to most of the Native American communities in the north and in the south. Actually the corn was a type of maize, seen elsewhere throughout the continent. Hardy, easily grown, corn (or maize) not only signified the renewal of the earth and its fertility, but announced the fact that the yearly time of plenty, the warm, quiet summer months, had arrived.

Corn, along with beans and squash, was called "our life," one of the "Three Sisters," or "our supporter" by the Iroquois. Tradition stated that corn sprouted from the breast of the mother of the Great Spirit when she died. Dances formed the normal style of celebration, including the famed and much prized Feather Dance, an elaborate ritual that boosted the morale of the people and joined them to the earth. On the third morning, after speeches and rituals, the people joined in choruses of song, listing all of the benefits which they had received from the earth, with the source being the Great Spirit. It must have been astounding for newcomers in the Iroquois lands to hear the great choir music soaring past the woodlands and rebounding in the river valleys.

The *Gus-ga' a*, the Peach-Stone Game, was also held, with sides rooting for their champions. The game was played in a bowl, which contained six peach pits. The pits were roasted on one side, to turn that surface black. Thus they appeared as black or white when they fell into the bowl. The trick was to jiggle the bowl enough to bounce the stones in such a way that at least five of the pits turned up in the same color. After the Peach-Stone Game and other contests, great helpings of succotash, the combination of corn, beans and squash, were served to the gathered masses.

The harvest Festival, called the *Da-yo-nun' -neo-qua Na De-o-Ha' ko*, was the last agricultural feast of the year, held after the harvests had been brought in throughout the Iroquois regions. Again, corn, beans and squash were honored as the staple crops, as the Three Sisters of bounty. The festival lasted four days and praised the Great Spirit for his generosity to humans on the earth. The celebration also honored nature itself, the source of all bounty. Dances were performed, and the festivities lasted normally until the first rays of the sun appeared on the horizon.

The ceremony with the greatest religious significance for the Iroquois was held in mid-winter, probably in February, and it was called *Gi' ye-wa-no-us-qua-go-wa*, or the New Year's Jubilee. The rituals of this feast lasted for seven days, incorporating all of the Iroquois religious ideals and all of the ancient traditions. Some of the more unique aspects of the ceremonies included the slaying of a White Dog and the interpretation of dreams. Like the Maple Dance and other feasts, this one was preceded by the "Meeting of Repentance," with special emphasis on the truthful recognition of one's faults and on a true spirit of repentance and reformation. Everything was geared to the beginning of yet another cycle in the seasonal march of nature, and on the anticipation of another year of life.

The Keepers of the Faith played significant roles in this celebration, visiting the homes of the clans, dressed in bear skins and buffalo robes, with corn-husk wreaths and corn-pounders in their hands. At each residence they advised the people to clean house, to discard trash and all useless items in preparation for the ceremonies. The New Year or Midwinter Festival was a fresh start for everyone. In a second visit, the elders announced the opening of the festivities and told the people to prepare the wooden blades used to stir ashes in the hearths of the various Longhouses. The White Dog, a sacred symbol, was then strangled, having been selected for its pure color and for its lack of blemishes. After strangulation and care that in the process no bone was broken and no blood spilled, the animal carcass was hung on a pole which was decorated for the occasion. On the fifth day it would be burned with rituals.

The second day of the New Year was a time for visiting among the Longhouses, and everyone put on their best clothes and went to spend time at the neighbors. The Keepers of the Faith were the first to make these ritual visits, and the houses were opened to the general populace only after the elders had made their calls. Throughout the day the Keepers of the Faith continued to make their social rounds, coming into each Longhouse three times. Other guests came and made a ceremonial gesture of stirring the ashes in their neighbors' hearths. All the time the people thanked the Great Spirit for having spared the households for another year.

On the following days dances were performed, and various forms of the sacred dances were held in different locations. Groups of young boys also went from Longhouse to Longhouse, pilfering what they could. If caught by an alert host, the items were returned immediately, if not, the owners of the various bits of property had to go redeem them at the close of the day.

Dreams were also part of the New Year Festival, as the Iroquois, along with other Native American communities, put stock in the dreams or visions which came to human beings over the years. Dream guessing was an activity that was popular, as one Indian would go about, describing his dreams until he received a satisfactory explanation from someone. The False Face Society, the Bear Society and the Husk Face Society members appeared, as did strange figures called "Big Heads." Games and athletic contests were sponsored, and sermons were given throughout the day.

The burning of the White Dog ended the Mid-Winter feast, and this was a serious and far-reaching ceremony for the people. The Keepers of the Faith and others admonished all gatherings to start anew and to make the New Year worthy of their efforts and their promises for renewal in faith. Babies were given names at this time, and the people enjoyed more dances and more games.

Thus the year ended with rejoicing and with an awareness of the gifts bestowed upon the people by the Great Spirit. Each year advanced in much the same way in the Iroquois villages, as the people used the celebrations and the rituals to bind them more closely to the earth. Kateri grew up amid these festivals, and three years after she was born, her mother gave birth to a son. The war chief and his family prospered, drawn into the richness of the spirit around them.

The propaganda of the films and the various histories concerning the Native American communities seldom explain or detail the very warm, kind and loving relationship that these people had for one another, traits very much evident in their abodes today. Indian women especially were loving with their children and attentive to their needs, carrying them about in the elaborately decorated papooses, crooning to them and seeing to their comfort. Kateri's mother must have spoken to her about the Christian faith, must have sang soft songs about the Christ and the saints. All around them was evidence of such faith, as the blood of the Jesuit martyrs had been spilled in Ossernenon a few years before.

The Jesuits, Isaac Jacques and John Lalande, both died horribly in the village in October 1646. In 1642 Rene Goupil had also perished there, along with French soldiers and with Huron captives. These deaths did not deter the missionaries from returning to the Mohawks, and the daring which they displayed in coming back into such potentially hostile lands must have won them admiration, even if given silently by the Mohawk people. The Five Nations maintained a certain tense balance with the French and their Indian allies, although the Mohawks, refusing to bend to the whims of foreign white men, did make raids on the settlements near or within their domain.

What Kateri's life would have been like with her family will never be known, as disaster struck her village and the Iroquois lands in 1660. The first sign of the impending tragedy came with the collapse of a Mohawk and the terrible display of the "purples" on his body. The "purples" as it was called because of the hideous rash that covered the skin, leaving permanent marks on those who recovered and signalling the ravages of the disease on the body as a whole, was the name given for smallpox. The disease was brought into Iroquois territories by the white men, and the Indians had absolutely no resistance to its dreaded toll.

As more and more sickened and died, the Iroquois medicine men and shamans performed their rituals, imploring the Great Spirit to put an end to the terrible suffering. More and more corpses were being carried from the Longhouses, and the disease struck young and old alike, leaving bands of mourners to wail over their dead. In the face of such a disease, the Iroquois were particularly helpless. Smallpox did not test the courage of a warrior or the resolve of an elderly matron. The healthiest looking among them, even those known for their bravery and honor, sickened and died without being able to summon the physical strength to combat this mortal foe. Fevers raged in the brains of the victims, as the "purples" spread across their bodies and shadows gathered about their pallets. In time the villagers became so alarmed and frantic that they began to murder the latest groups of captives brought home by their warriors. Men died screaming in the village square, even as women and children gasped out their last in the darkened alcoves of the Longhouses.

Kateri caught the disease, and she was put on her pallet and nursed by the village women who despaired of her life. Her mother could not care for her, as she lay dead with her small son in her arms. Even Kateri's father, the great war chief of the village, suffered and slipped away from them all. The village mourned, and the sound of the dogs wailing and the women keening over their loved ones echoed through the woods and the plains.

In time, of course, the epidemic had run its course, dying out naturally as the disease is wont to do in all lands. Kateri recovered slowly, but she was heavily pock-marked, and her eyes no longer had their merry lights or their loveliness. She was half blind, reduced to seeing all creatures in shadows. The sun especially hurt her eyes and made her cringe and seek the darkness.

With the death of the great war chief, the village matriarchs had to gather to elect his replacement, and they chose his brother, listed by one source as a warrior named Iowerano. A fierce man, just and set on maintaining the old ways among his people, he moved into the Longhouse in his brother's place, bringing his wife and an aunt with him. The care of Kateri was given to them, as it was proper for them to raise a dead brother's child, particularly a young woman of such an exalted rank. He appears to have favored Kateri from the start, perhaps entranced by the shyness which developed after the illness, perhaps recalling the great admonitions which the Five Nations' founding documents declared about the care of the weak, the aged, and the orphaned. Contemporaries said that Kateri had very lovely features, as well as a charming smile. Her skin would ever remain rather swarthy and pock-marked, but such disfigurements did not dismay the Indians as they did the white men. Adopting Kateri was proper for Iowerano, but it was also a shrewd political move on his part. He did not have children of his own apparently, and this daughter would eventually attract a fine warrior who would enter the household and carry on the lineage of Iowerano's family. The wife, listed by one source as being named Karitha, welcomed the child lovingly, as did the aunt, Arsone.

At the end of the plague, when the dead had been placed in their resting places, the villagers decided to leave the area. The Iroquois had several ways of honoring their dead, including a special festival in which the remains of previously buried corpses were gathered and moved to a common grave site. In this manner the skeletons of whole families were perpetually cared for and never abandoned. The religious beliefs of the Iroquois stated that the journey from earth to heaven took the soul many days. Families often held services at the end of a year, exchanging their mourning cries for rejoicing, as they believed their loved one had reached his or her ultimate destination in heaven. Later Iroquois lessened the time of the soul's journey. While Kateri lived, the Iroquois captured a bird and freed it over the grave of a loved one on the evening of the burial so that the creature could bear the soul upward to its rest. Most of the corpses were buried with their personal things, including bows and arrows, tobacco and pipes and food for the journey. The body was painted and dressed in the finest clothes, and a fire was provided at the grave during the night so that the deceased could cook its food and be comfortable.

No doubt the families of Ossernenon gathered up the remains of their relatives and ancestors as the village began to disassemble the various residences and to pack up the belongings of each clan. Ossernenon was now a site of unhappiness, of bad memories, perhaps even of contagion, and the people felt it was better to head toward Auries' Creek, to start the new village of Gandawague. All of them prayed that one day the new generations would return to this lovely place, to restore it and to return it to its traditions. In the meantime, however, it was better for them to start again where the water was clean and pure, and where the forests rang only with the sounds of animals and birds. Kateri and her warrior chief uncle looked back to Ossernenon, but then they turned and went with the villagers toward their new home.

Unlike the American Plains Indians, those tribes that followed the seasons and roamed the wilderness in search of game or sheltering havens in the times of winter storms, the Iroquois were normally residents of permanent villages which were constructed with defensive works and placed in strategically advantageous sites. Trenches were built around the towns, usually several feet deep. Within the perimeters of these trenches, there were rows of stakes and palisades that inclined over the trenches so that enemies would be impaled during their charges. Some Iroquois villages were surrounded by several rows of these palisades and stakes. Such fortifications were not necessary in all of the Iroquois territories, because their power had been consolidated and their position made secure. The Mohawks and the Oneidas, however, within range of the invading white men and their Indian allies, took pains to maintain forts.

The white men appeared early on the Iroquois domains, and the Five Nations became tolerant of some and sworn enemies of others. The Dutch started a trading post at Orange, modern Albany, sometime in 1615, proving cautious and considerate neighbors to the Indians. They well understood the nature of the Iroquois and respected their power. The Five Nations had subdued tribes throughout the region and were sophisticated in matters of diplomacy and government. Actually, the Iroquois expelled the Native Americans living in the Niagara Peninsula as early as 1643. By 1653 they had nearly decimated the Eries and had control of New York and northern Ohio. By 1670 they had conquered the Hurons and the Algonquins, called Adirondacks in some accounts, and they controlled the fur trade and the tribal affairs in New York, Delaware, Maryland, New Jersey, Pennsylvania, northern Virginia, northeastern Ohio, Kentucky, and parts of Illinois, Indiana, Michigan and Canada. Over these tribes the Iroquois kept close watch, and when problems arose they sent a large military force under the command of chiefs, who gave counsel and took steps necessary to insure Iroquois domination.

The Iroquois found the Dutch circumspect and careful, and they became friendly with the English as well when Britain took over the Dutch lands in 1664. They traded furs for arms and other equipment and established a "covenant chain" that they kept until the American Revolution. The Dutch and the English kept to themselves, tried not to interfere in Indian affairs and treated the chiefs with respect and caution. The Iroquois, in return, treated them tolerantly and allowed a certain amount of trade to flourish between the groups.

Not so with the French. To begin with, the French were in Montreal, which the Iroquois called their spiritual or ancestral home. As early as 1609, when Champlain, the French explorer, entered the region of the lake that would one day bear his name, the Iroquois took up arms against all French intruders. From 1640 until 1700, in fact, there was constant warfare between the French and the Iroquois. The two groups fought over the St. Lawrence River and Lake Erie and Lake Ontario, a region that was rich in pelts and game. The French were unable to trap or hunt in the area and eventually had to go up the Ottawa River, cross to Sault Ste. Marie and then use the Lake Superior territories for their trapping. This was intolerable, as the infant French colonies depended upon furs.

In order to settle the situation, the French used Huron and Algonquin allies and tried to manage diplomatic agreements. The Iroquois proved far too sophisticated for the French, who could only mutter vague promises and offer treaties that gave the Indians little advantage. They tried wars but the Iroquois could field vast armies and were military tacticians who struck terrible blows and then vanished. At times, the Iroquois allowed the French to ravage a particular town or village, staying hidden and untouchable while the natural elements and the frustration of never having a decisive meeting drove the French into retreat. In the meantime, the Iroquois, especially the Mohawks, attacked French settlements and wreaked havoc up and down the borders. Finally, in 1665, Courcelles, the Governor of Canada, led a campaign against the Mohawks with the hope of crushing them forever. The Governor and his troops were forced to withdraw after suffering untold hardships in the wilderness. This campaign would be followed by a more compelling one, led by De Tracy, with the Carignan Regiment and the Canadian militia in 1667. That campaign would have a direct effect on the life of Kateri Tekakwitha.

While these battles and raids raged in the French and Iroquois lands, the villagers continued their own routines, and Kateri's family and clan members moved from Ossernenon to Aurics' Creek, to the settlement called Gandawague (modern Caughnawaga/Kahnawake Reserve). It was a time-consuming effort that entailed many labors and had to be fully supported by everyone of the community. The Longhouses at Ossernenon had to be stripped of their bark and pelts, and the poles were removed for use elsewhere. The belongings of each hearth family were packed up and carried to the new site, and the stored food supplies had to be retrieved from the pits and silos. The families normally gathered up the remains of their ancestral dead as well, taking them to the new village for reburial.

On the site of Gandawague, the people had to decide upon the defensive position — close enough to the water for use and yet distant enough to avoid ambushes or sneak attacks by canoes — and the elders had to select the best side of the creek and the proper hill for fortifications. Not only the French were raiding in the Mohawk territories, but the Mohicans were also sending in small parties to harrass and damage the various town populations.

The women of the village, with the help of the men in certain stages of building, were the ones responsible for erecting the

Longhouses. In some towns the individual families resided separately during some eras of Iroquoian history, but normally these Longhouses were structured to accommodate as many as twenty families within each residence. Clans lived there together, supporting the individual hearth families.

Kateri was still small and rather weak when the move was made, so perhaps she did not perform many tasks, but all Mohawk children were expected to do their share when the community was involved in a project. As she was growing in strength and in age, however, her chores increased accordingly. In her young years she was considered quite amiable and intelligent by her relatives and neighbors, who took delight in her skills in decorating items of clothing. She was taught to use beads and quills to fashion exquisite designs, and her eyesight was apparently of a nature that allowed her to do the embroidery work close at hand. The traditional Mohawk designs were favored, but Kateri was known for inventing lovely ones of her own.

Her own clothes were stylish and elegant, made for her by the loving hands of her aunts. The women of her clan took particular pride in dressing her according to her rank in the village. These women loved elaborate patterns, and they wore jewelry of all kinds, probably because such bits of finery distracted them from the day to day routines. Kateri's hair was plaited and interwoven with small ornaments, and her blouses, skirts and leggings were fashioned out of the softest hides, beautifully treated, and brightened by the use of vivid colors. When the winter months came, she wore a mantle of red wool, or perhaps of brown, and her mocassins were elaborately decorated as well. The Mohawks also wore snowshoes, woven out of bark, reeds and other natural materials. Such snowshoes allowed them to travel across the terrain even in the cruelest months of the year.

For a good many years, Kateri's life was a normal one according to the village standards, and she was certainly enmeshed in the tender and loving embrace of her new family. She was always sweet tempered and willing to work, although she shied from village dances and festivities because of her eye problems. This isolation served as a bridge between the village life and the waiting landscape of the mystical soul, where graces were at work within her. Perhaps it was the influence of her gentle mother, who must have remained as a dim memory in her mind, caught in images, in sounds, even in vaguely remembered words that came rushing out of the past. Kateri was the product of the American wilderness, the daughter of the proud Mohawk clans, but she yearned within her for another type of life, for another union that was foreign and hidden in her early life.

As she matured, Kateri was given many of the domestic duties of the hearth as part of her daily schedule, something which made life easier for her because it spared her the company of young people her own age and allowed her to nurture the spirit of solitude, which had become so much a part of her nature. Mohawk women were charged normally with bringing drinking and cooking water from the nearby river or stream, gathering the wood for fires, as well as hunting for small game, for nuts, berries and honey. Kateri pounded corn for several hours each day, making the flour so necessary to the cooking. She also helped prepare animal skins that were brought proudly into the village by the Woodland Warriors. She became particularly adept at making headbands, embroidering pouches, leggings, shirts, skirts and the bags used by the warriors and the women. Kateri also worked on the wampum belts, the bands formed out of beads and shells, used for ceremonial and governmental purposes.

During her formative years, Kateri probably underwent a Mohawk ritual which was bound to the marriage traditions of the Five Nations. Marriage among the Iroquois was seldom based on a sudden passion or a desire between two individuals. Most marriage contracts were drawn up by the elder women of the villages, who saw to it that the couple was not closely linked by blood ties, shared ranks and status and came from families that would be reasonably compatible in the future. The status of sons-in-law was critical, and many vied to obtain brides from the better residences and clans, so as to enter them and become part of a higher ranked social strata. It has been reported that many Mohawk children were espoused at an early age, probably oblivious to the ramifications of the ceremonies when they were dressed in their finery and pledged to one another in the presence of the matriarchs. The children sometimes married but could also end up wed to others in time. The original espousal at young ages was intended to cement ties between families and to put into place a framework for future unions.

In the earlier days, Mohawk youths were not married until they reached maturity, approximately twenty five years of age, and then many were wed to older women, who served as stabilizing influences. In Kateri's time, however, the couples were closer to one another's age. The pairs seldom had the opportunity of discovering one another before they were betrothed, as young warriors could not just go up to any maiden to carry on conversations. Certainly they managed to flirt and to make their feelings known, but the marriage contracts were not based on anything as trivial as physical attractions.

As Kateri grew older, her aunts decided that it was time for her to consider marriage. If she went through a childhood espousal, it is not recorded, but she was nearing the age for marriage, and the women of the village began making plans. Her physical disfigurement meant very little because she was a chieftain's daughter, the adopted daughter of another war chief, and she was known as being amiable, industrious and talented. When she refused to even discuss marriage, the aunts wondered if Kateri's Algonquin, Christian mother had not bequeathed strange ideas to her child.

The aunts and the other elder women did not debate the matter with Kateri, allowing her to continue her solitary existence, with its long hours in the hearth area of the Longhouse or out on the country trails. Kateri did not act obstinately, did not close the door on the subject — just put off all discussions — the women set themselves to remedying the situation in their own fashion. One of the acts of accepting a spouse was that of serving him food. Knowing this, the women invited a very eligible young man to the Longhouse, and he came willingly, content that he had received an invitation not only to Kateri's bed but to membership in the prestigious clan.

After the first awkward moments of conversation, one of Kateri's aunts asked her to serve the young warrior a bowl of sagamite, a type of porridge. Kateri, however, quite alert to the various aspects of the marriage ceremony, rose from her place and went out of the Longhouse to walk alone in the woods. The astonished young man, refused so bluntly, left the residence, and the women sat and discussed the strange turn of events.

It must be remembered that these matriarchs were functioning in accordance with the dictates of their own traditions. They belonged to a people whose safety rested in numbers, especially in the propagation of healthy, sturdy children who could carry on the nation's affairs when the elders passed on to the Great Spirit and made their journey to heaven. The duty of every female was to marry and to bear children for the good of the family, the clan, the nation and the Confederacy. Nowhere was there any admonition about people remaining virginal. The god of the Iroquois did not request a group of dedicated people to live apart from the rest in order to serve him. Kateri's refusal to even discuss marriage was thus alien, strange and perhaps even dangerous to the Mohawk way of life. Certainly the women could not come up with a good reason for her to refuse to accept her share of the nation's obligations. Each one of them was raised to know his or her place in the scheme of things, as each one was taught to assume the duties of his or her station and to perform them in gratitude and reverence to the Great Spirit and to the ancestors.

The aunts and the other matriarchs were naturally at a loss to explain her peculiar aversion to the marriage bed, and they began to devise ways in which to bring Kateri to her senses. She had not shown any indication of being Christian, as her mother had been, and she had not talked with priests as far as anyone knew. Since the plot against the Blackrobes in 1658, no missionaries had come into the land. If Kateri was not a Christian, she was being strong willed and selfish. If she hid Christian sentiments, she was going against the good of the nation as decreed by the elders. In either case she had to be punished and made to see reason.

Actually, Kateri was a Christian, but one of the unique souls called by God to a life of mystical union. The Mohawks were well aware of the conversions being made among the Native Americans by the diligent French Jesuits. Everywhere one heard of the Christian faith and of the havens of Christianity being established in the wilderness. The Christian teachings did not come as alien concepts to the Iroquois, whose own religious ideals prepared them for the fullness of faith. The covenants recognized between the individual and the Great Spirit had long been hallowed and taught among the various nations, and now even chiefs were beginning to discover the faith as the ultimate way for those whom the Great Spirit had long favored. Kateri knew about Christianity. She was weaned on the gentle ways of Jesus, the Savior, her inheritance from her mother, and she knew that the blood of martyrs had been spilled in her birthplace, Ossernenon. Now she listened as others spoke of the conversions and the new way of life which was coming into Iroquois lands. If she did not speak of such things to her relatives, that was because of her modest nature and because she was allowing the news to become implanted and nurtured by grace deep within her.

Her refusal to even discuss marriage with a young warrior, and her quickness in recognizing the ruse being played on her by her aunts, give indications of an intelligent appraisal of her life and of her ultimate spiritual goals. Her refusal earned her the enmity of the clan women, however, and from that day forward she was to face harsh treatment at their hands. She was laughed at, mocked for her failings and given the most demeaning of the household tasks. Kateri was no longer the beloved daughter, the one to be dressed in finery and shown before the young warriors. She took on the status of a slave in her residence. Faced with such hostility and unkindness, however, she imitated her mother in captivity, and met all acts with gentleness and a sweet smile. This attitude upset the women of the clan, who actually liked her, and in time they gave up trying to force her into the arms of some willing warrior. The matriarchs were caught between their affection for this docile, winning maiden and their eagerness to see the Mohawk way of life endure in the world, despite changes, challenges and disasters.

The village affairs were cast aside actually in the year 1667, when the French forces, under the command of De Tracy, the Viceroy of New France, attacked the Mohawk domain once again. A Marquis, De Tracy led the famed Carignan Regiment as well as Canadian militia and Indian allies in the campaign. Entering the Mohawk territories, they burned and ravaged the crops and the residences and then withdrew when meeting no opposition. The long term result, however, was a treaty between the Iroquois and the French, with adequate provisions for fur trading, safe conduct and a general peace. The treaty lasted eighteen years, and it was but one of a long line of pacts and contracts made by the diplomatic Iroquois over the centuries. These men were skilled at such bargaining and diplomatic relationships, and they entered into them with enthusiasm and eloquence.

Many of the Five Nations member groups had long considered the prospects of making peace with the French, which would include putting an end to the enmity between the Iroquois and the Hurons and Algonquins. There were certainly advantages in undertaking an end to hostilities on the white man's borders, not the least of which would be a period in which the Iroquois could consolidate their holdings and train their own forces for any future outbreaks. The presence of the white man was no longer an issue which could be avoided. There were too many of them, and combined with the political institutions which the various groups were putting in place, the Iroquois were becoming vulnerable. It was obvious that these Europeans had every intention of subduing the region around their original sites, and they would arrange such subjugation with or without war.

The Mohawks, of course, had held out against such compromise, having borne the brunt of the French assaults and having the greatest enmity against the white men and their allies. After the 1667 campaign, however, the wise chiefs among the Mohawks listened to the prudent counsels of others and decided to accept the terms of peace which were being offered to them. Like the other Indian nations in the region, they too were beginning to understand the inevitability of the white man's invasion into their land. The Mohawk region, long held in stewardship and in gratitude by the "Flint Possessing People," the *Ga'ne'a-ga-o-no*, as Kateri's clans called themselves, was becoming inundated by alien people that coveted the forests, the streams and the pristine wilderness. Like a contagious plague, these white men were stealing into their woods, across their meadows and into the very fiber of the wilds. With the others of the Five Nations, the Mohawks consented to a truce, which would endure for a significant period, considering the difficulties presented on both sides.

The Mohawks even consented to allow the Blackrobes, the missionaries, back into their lands. They did not accept them with much enthusiasm deep within their hearts, because these eager, devoted men represented the inexorable changes that were coming to the Land of the Longhouses. The first missionaries had died at the hands of the Mohawks, and it was perhaps a bit surprising to them that the new group of Blackrobes would be willing to endanger themselves once again. Three Jesuits, Father Jacques Fremin, Father Jean Pierron and Father Jacques Bruyas, were blessed by Bishop Laval in June, 1677, accepting whatever fate lay in wait for them among the Mohawks and the rest of the Five Nations Confederacy.

The unanimous decision of the Five Nations' Sachems, representing the pooled resources of the Iroquois as a whole, normally held sway and enforced a code of behavior over the participating members. The peace treaty with the French followed that same pattern. So did the entrance of the Blackrobes into the Mohawk region. The missionaries were greeted with considerable ceremony when they arrived. Even Kateri's uncle, despite his reservations, courteously played host to the newcomers. His own longhouse was put at their disposal, because that was part of the honorable treatment to be afforded the Blackrobes. Certainly her uncle was not suffering from a change of heart where Catholicism or the missionaries were concerned. He had deep resentments against their particular spiritual viewpoints, and he distrusted all white men because of the perfidy with which the Mohawks and other Native Americans had been met in the past. The chief was aided in this opinion by his alliance with the nearby British, as well, as these people detested the French and viewed the "Papism" that the Jesuits taught with scorn. The English made no attempt to convert any of the Native Americans with whom they came in contact. Like the Dutch before them, they saw no pressing need for saving souls. The French, by contrast, constantly worried about the Iroquois, who were living without benefit of the true faith and the sacraments. This devotion was so strong, in fact, that they were willing to die in order to bring the "Good News," the Gospel, into the villages of the Five Nations.

The first missionaries who had been blessed by Bishop Laval, were asked later about their first encounter with Kateri Tekakwitha. They stated that they remembered that visit, having experienced her modesty and gentleness, something that was quite unlike the normal Mohawk young woman of the time. One termed her behavior as possessing "a sweet docility" as she carried out the orders of her powerful uncle. Kateri, along with the other members of the household, served the guests, bringing the bowls of sagamite porridge and arranging the sleeping pallets and the fires. She said very little to the guests, as she was normally shy and retiring, but she did dare to inquire as to how long the missionaries planned to remain in the region.

The priests probably thought that she was showing a courteous interest in their affairs, because they had no way of knowing what was taking place within her young heart and soul. They also had no inkling of the "treasure" that was present in their midst. She remained hidden, growing in the presence of God and with the graces of the Holy Spirit, which trained and formed her spiritual attributes. Kateri did not ask an idle question. She had longed for the sight of the priests, as she had longed for another force to overwhelm her nature.

The third landscape of Kateri Tekakwitha's life thus entered the scene, compliments of the French eagerness to get their hands on furs and lands. The Blackrobes were French, but they did not share in the avarice or determination of their political counterparts among their own kind. They only benefited from the gains made by the armies and the negotiators of New France, enabled to travel at last among the Confederacy and to begin the work for which they had been trained. They were Jesuits, after all, one of the most dedicated and uniquely prepared religious orders within the Catholic Church, who had been drawn to the Rule of St. Ignatius Loyola, had caught the fire of the early fathers and burned for the salvation of souls.

The Jesuit order was founded only a century before yet, as missionaries, they represented centuries of martyrs and mystics, saints and scholars, and the tradition of safeguarding the faith in pagan outposts around the world. Such men, and the women religious who joined them in this great undertaking, had survived the rank barbarism and disasters of the Dark Ages, had built countless edifices of worship through the Middles Ages and had maintained the Church through the sprawling heathenism of the Renaissance in Europe. Above all, these Blackrobes came armed with the sacraments of the Church, with the presence of Christ, and with the doctrines that would become the framework of a new life for thousands in the American wilderness. If the doors were opened to them by French greed and political cunning, by the introduction of terrible new weapons of war, the result of their efforts would bridge the centuries again and would offer men and women of the New World a startling and salvific vision of eternity.

Kateri mildly inquired as to how long the priests intended to remain in the area, but her soul was asking for considerably more. They replied that they were there only briefly. As it turned out, however, a chapel was erected in Gandawague (Caughnawaga/Kahnawake Reserve), and a missionary was stationed within calling distance of the young maiden. The Blackrobes also invested five new missions, a contract guaranteed by the treaty with the French. These missions were started at:

- Tionnontaguen — Ste. Marie Mission (in the Mohawk capital)
- Onneyout — St. Francis Xavier Mission (in the Oneida lands)
- Onnontaque — St. John the Baptist Mission (in Onondaga lands)
- Gayoquin — St. Joseph Mission (in Cayuga lands)
- Tsannontouan — St. Michael Mission (in Seneca lands)

Father John Pierron, S.J., was stationed in the Mohawk village of Kateri's clans at first. It must have been stressful and difficult in the opening days, despite his love for the Iroquois, as he was now after all in the vicinity of the very people who had slain his pious predecessors. He was unable to speak the Iroquois language, as there had not been enough communication between the French and the Five Nations to allow the missionary to learn the tongue. Also, the treaty had been hoped for, but few believed that the Confederacy would accept such terms.

In order to overcome this rather critical shortcoming, Father Pierron used his innate artistic skills and his vivid imagination. He painted elaborate and striking scenes and symbols on pieces of linen in order to depict visually the truths that he was attempting to give to the people. Such artistic renditions, naturally, attracted the Mohawks, who were quite adept at artistic endeavors themselves and were affected by beauty and by harmony of design. The presentation of the paintings caused a stir at first and then was followed by what the priest called the game of "point to point." Through the pictures and symbols, he demonstrated the progress of each human being from the cradle to the grave.

Now all of this was rather inventive and astute, but Father Pierron had no idea of the wellspring of traditions into which he was tapping with his artwork and his game. The Iroquois vision of life and death corresponded to much of what he showed them, and he discovered that they understood much of what he was trying to convey in his performances. The Five Nations had long lived with the view that the human sojourn on the earth was a time of testing for each individual, a time in which duties were to be performed and gifts were to be shared for the good of all. The Great Spirit also symbolized the creative, nurturing and just authority of God. Such beliefs were already dominant and ingrained in the people, thus the "point to point" exercises proved particularly effective and opened the door to conversion in many.

Father Pierron worked endlessly among the Mohawks, baptizing children and the dying while instructing the adults of the villages. He and his fellow Jesuits were extremely cautious about administering the sacraments to mature Mohawks who were in good health. Such conversions not only brought about the enmity of the pagans but endangered the entire apostolate as well. Adult converts had to be trained over a period of months, and the reception of baptism was held as a reward for constancy, endurance and a change of life as well as of attitude. This sort of caution stemmed from a fear of apostasy among the newly converted. Apostates in the tribes, those who turned their backs on the Church and the faith when angered or sorely tried, proved most often the most vicious enemies of the priests in the long run. By forcing the adults to undergo tedious and detailed catechetical instructions before conversion, the priests also allowed themselves the necessary time for discovering the individuals on a personal basis. They could make inquiries as to the moral fiber and the spiritual health of the convert too. The Indians lived so close together in their longhouses that few secrets could be kept, especially from the Keepers of the Faith or the astute matriarchs. While instructing the adults, Father Pierron also tried to influence the lifestyle of the Mohawks. He constantly urged them to refrain from the use of alcohol, the "firewater" that the English and others provided so willingly. Even Kateri's uncle had to concur with this viewpoint, as he recognized the danger in the use of such substances.

The uncle, however, was not won over by Father Pierron. He had yet another reason for distrusting the Jesuits and their teachings, and in this bias he was demonstrating the traditional wisdom of the Five Nations Confederacy. Many of the Iroquois who became Christians abandoned their tribes and their home villages in order to live on a more spiritualized plane in the Mission of St. Francis Xavier at La Prairie, on the St. Lawrence River. The establishment was called the Sault Mission in time, as it was moved to Sault St. Louis. There the Indians could live in peace, following their Christian ideals and attending the various services performed there by the resident priests. In 1670, Father Pierron was taken from Kateri's village and replaced by Father Francis Boniface.

This missionary, adept at languages, actually skilled in the American tongues that he discovered, was able to converse with the Iroquois. He became more and more familiar with the language as he lived among them, approaching the vocabulary and pronunciation as a scholar. In time he set about translating the prayers of the Mass, the hymns and the catechisms into the Mohawk tongue. Hearing the Catholic prayers and devotions in their own language, of course, had a profound effect upon the people. The Iroquois gift of oratory, the elegance of their discourses and imagery, and the continued use of the language on an almost classical level, allowed the people to recognize clarity, beauty and eloquence in another form of worship. The prayers, hymns and canons which had developed over the centuries in the Church, therefore, had an impact upon them.

Father Boniface also provided the people with a marvelous form of worship which was familiar to them from their own traditions. He translated the Christian hymns into Iroquois and taught the parishioners how to chant the ageless praises. Everyday, in fact, the Christians and other curious or interested parties gathered around the altar of the mission to intone the hymns, sending a great paean of joy into the forests and fields. Just as they had sung the songs of praise in the *Ah-dake' wa-o*, the Festival of the Green Corn, so did the Mohawks join in harmony to celebrate the new faith that had been brought to them. The woods and valleys echoed not just on holy days or on the agricultural feast days but everyday. Many non-Christians were attracted to the choruses, naturally, and they gathered to listen or to sing along with their neighbors. In time, Father Boniface trained a children's choir as well, which delighted the people of the region.

Kateri did not belong to that choir, and she did not make herself known at any of the songfests or services. Hidden, distant and almost like a shadow, she absorbed every detail of the new doctrines, listened to the hymns and to the sentiments that they evoked in their melodies. There were discussions about the Black-robes throughout the camp, and the women and the elders debated again and again the doctrinal points which Boniface was making in their own language.

At Christmas, Father Boniface scored a major victory with the villagers. He provided a display that won their hearts and brought them into the ranks of millions. The display was the creche, the manger scene, used with such effectiveness in days past by St. Francis of Assisi. This manger, this representation of the birth of Christ, was totally Iroquois in design and structure, and it bridged their world with the alien one of the faith. The chapel itself was decorated with pine bows, pelts, feathers, and other ornaments, and the crib was surrounded by branches, ribbons and lovely beads. A statue of the Christ Child, the Prince of Peace, was placed in the crib, and he stretched out his small arms to the people from the foot of the altar. The Mohawks came in great numbers, naturally, to see such a charming sign of Christmas, as they loved their children and appreciated the significance of the Babe in the lowly bed of the stable. Such a scene related to their own natural world, to their concept of man and the earth, and it conveyed the doctrines of the Church clearly.

In this demonstration, Father Boniface hit upon the basic elements of the Native American aversion to the faith in the past. They resented all things European, even as they might be awed by them, and they certainly did not understand the need for elaborate churches, gilded shrines and stilted, formal rituals. They had long felt the presence of their Great Spirit in the natural settings, in the rapturously beautiful mountains and valleys, in the icy streams and the still wilderness. This crib, with the Christ Child opening his arms to embrace the world, would have struck a chord in their hearts, as it has touched the lives of countless millions over the centuries. On this "Silent Night" the Mohawks discovered the same spirit of Christmas that transforms the people of the earth once a year into "men of good will" who desire peace.

For Kateri the Christ Child would have symbolized something far more profound. Her heart and soul, shadowed and emptied of everything for so long, ached for the enduring, everlasting and ultimate espousal. She was not merely looking for someone to love. She could have found that easily enough in one of the many young warriors of the nation. She was not looking for comfort or ease in a relationship, as she had many offers of kindness and compassion from those around her, even those who did not understand her strange ideals or her retiring ways. Kateri was unique in the fact that she glimpsed, even untutored, the vastness of Divine Love, and she felt the emanations of that Love surging through the wilderness and into her life. She sought the Divine Spouse, but only because that Beautiful Prince of Peace had sought her first.

If she was able to spend time contemplating the image of the Christ Child is not known. Certainly she heard the hymns and the gentle sentiments that washed over the village as the Christmas season was celebrated by the mission. The manger would have drawn her, bedazzled her and urged her into the realm of prayer. The decorations, even the image of the Holy Babe were not the ultimate lures. Instead, she recognized the Divine Presence symbolized by the display, and this Presence began to permeate her life. She was already docile, modest, retiring and unassuming. Now she was discovering that a human soul can be enraptured, caught up in a mystical embrace in the midst of the common, ordinary aspects of everyday living. The landscapes of Kateri's life were blending, circling, spiraling outward, one on top of another, as the choirs of angels radiated out from the throne of the Unbegotten Father.

By 1673, Father Boniface had converted approximately thirty adults in a village of 300 Mohawks. He was aided in this by the appearance of a remarkable man called the "Great Mohawk" in his own nation: Kryn. Kryn was a chief of the nation, a convert to the faith and a man of eloquence and untiring devotion. He lived at Sault Mission, which he described to the new Christians as a paradise of love and faith, where one and all — even those of enemy tribes — could live in harmony and in service to the Lord. The image was quite compelling, especially for those who were devout and experiencing intolerance among their family members and friends. As Kateri's uncle had long feared, some forty Mohawks asked to leave Gandawague in order to reside in their new faith at Mission Sault. Kryn was delighted, and Father Boniface agreed to the journey, leading his converts there personally. He returned to the village and continued working but died suddenly on December 17, 1674.

It is not known if Father Boniface had any inkling as to Kateri's spirituality during his ministry in the region. She was rapidly maturing, despite her isolation and lonely way of life, and she was already demonstrating some of the hallmarks of the mystics and truly heroic souls. She remained serene despite hardships, thirsting always for union with God and yet willing to wait until he opened the way for her to come into his arms through the sacraments. Never allowing herself to repay a cruelty with the same spirit, she endured in all things and lived as a docile instrument in his hands; an amiable and pliable approach demonstrated by some of Christendom's most exalted spiritual giants in the past. She was also learning enough about the sufferings of Christ to know that hers were quite trivial in comparison. Taking the bits of catechetical instruction that were made available to her, Kateri began to set a high standard of perfection for herself, even without the joy and comfort of being able to declare herself publicly as a follower of Christ and the Cross. The Cross, in fact, became her insignia long before she was anointed with holy oils and given entrance into the Kingdom of God's Chosen.

The replacement sent by the Jesuits for Father Boniface was heaven-sent as far as Kateri Tekakwitha was concerned. Actually, Father Jacques de Lamberville stands as a representative of a truly unique group of pioneers in the American missions, one of countless numbers of dedicated priests who endured all things for the love of Christ and for the love of human souls. America can boast a remarkable cast of such missionaries, who entered the wilderness, worked there and died unsung, except in the hearts of the local people. The French Jesuits, the Sulpicians, the Franciscans, the Sacred Heart Fathers, and numerous other priests from the European cradles of the faith, served without complaint to Christianize the New World. While it is fashionable now to relate their deeds to the changing social concepts, placing them in a context of modern, more enlightened approaches, they stand alone and unsullied in their efforts. If they believed that their charges were naive, unprepared for the changing world, and if they brought with them the European ideas about white dominance and white supremacy, they did so because they were products of their own eras. It is quite easy for people to minimize and diminish their labors now with slogans and claims of new humanistic awareness. That sort of historical consideration, however, is equally as biased and unfair as the one they attach to the missionaries of America's early days. Each generation functions according to its own lights, according to its own traditions. The missionaries of the young America transcended their prejudices and preconceived notions about the place of the Native Americans, and in the end they were willing to give their lives for their flocks, which is probably more than can be said for their modern detractors.

Father Jacques de Lamberville was known to the Mohawks, who named him "Dawn of Day." He was a scholar as well as a missionary, and he was one of two brothers sent into the American territories. Jean de Lamberville, who spent 23 years among the Iroquois, was his sibling. This priest was recalled to Paris finally to become the Procurator of the Canadian Missions, thus insuring that a veteran of the wilderness, a man who was aware of the problems and challenges, was able to conduct the ministerial affairs. Jacques remained always in the New World, serving thirty years among the people of the Longhouses, among the Five Nations of the Iroquois. He was also the guiding light for the neophyte mystic, Kateri Tekakwitha.

Father de Lamberville took up his post when Father Boniface died, and he labored in the village, accustomed to missionary assignments and to the various duties entailed in such a role. He was a prudent man, but he was also astute and aware of the great variations available to human souls in their union with Almighty God. His scholarly background and his experience in the field provided him with that perspective.

He worked in the village but did not speak to Kateri for some time. Certainly he must have seen her in passing, perhaps even noticing her standing like a shadow at the Christian festivities. Kateri's life was more peaceful at the time, but she felt constrained and unable to express herself publicly. Then, one day, when passing Kateri's longhouse residence, the priest felt impelled to enter. He did not expect to find anyone, as the Mohawks were industrious and did not spend a great deal of time in their homes during the day, although many of the women's duties were set in the residences.

Entering the house, Father de Lamberville discovered Kateri there, being visited by two Indian maidens. She had wounded her foot somehow and was propped up on her pallet, listening to the tales that her guests spun for her amusement. It seems as if the controversy over her refusal to marry had dimmed somewhat. The Mohawk women were practical, and they did not waste time trying to prolong arguments with obstinate youngsters. Time, they knew, was a great healer and brought more than one hot-headed child into line. Also, the unique sense of justice which prevailed in the Mohawk community, especially among the matriarchs, would have soothed the situation. Kateri had given no further offense, had not retaliated in any way for the treatment that she had received. This amiability, this willingness to pay the price for her particular viewpoint, would have won the hearts of her aunts and the matriarchs.

When Kateri saw Father de Lamberville in her residence, she welcomed him warmly and began to talk to him of the things that were in her heart. Despite the presence of the other women, she spoke of her parents, of her Christian mother, and of her knowledge of the Catholic faith. Then, without any hesitation, Kateri announced that she would like to become a Christian.

True to his Jesuit training and to his experiences over the years in the American wilderness, Father de Lamberville did not discourage her from becoming a convert, but he did not rush into the situation either. If he was stunned by her advanced prayer life, which she made known to him, he did not make mention of it. As a wise counselor he urged her to continue in her prayers and in learning about the faith. He had no intention of welcoming her to baptism without the usual indoctrination program, no matter how bright and gifted she appeared. In fact, her precocious knowledge about the faith and the spiritual life may have sounded an alarm in his mind. She had the makings of a gifted soul, one specially called, but he could not take a chance on her endurance. She was the daughter of one chief, the adopted ward of another, and as such she carried considerable rank in the Mohawk nation. She needed to undergo the same treatment as the other adult converts, perhaps more so, because she would be an example for good or for ill among her own people. He was probably relieved when she showed no disappointment about being treated like everyone else. Kateri would appear for regular catechetical lessons and would attend the services along with the other newly converted Christians.

She began instructions without opposition from her uncle or other family members, probably because they felt that she needed something in her life to draw her out of her solitude. Certainly Christianity was well established in the village by that time, a natural part of the routine there, so there was no purpose in denying Kateri something that others had willingly embraced. Her uncle cautioned her to be discreet and extremely prudent in her dealings with the priests and the other converts. She carried considerable rank and could bring about situations without realizing their ramifications or their lasting effects. He did not forbid her to take instructions, and he did not make any effort to change her mind, having discovered that she could be as obstinate as he was.

Kateri thus began her "point to point" studies, having advanced interiorly far beyond that stage but demonstrating again her unique docility. It did not much matter how she attained baptism and entry into the Church, after all, and being allowed to openly proclaim herself a follower of Christ was worth any delay or prolonged study. Father de Lamberville met with her and explained Catholic doctrine and traditions. He also went about the village making discreet inquiries as to the character and personality of this new convert. No one complained about her character at all. They thought she was a bit odd, and they certainly still smarted at her refusal to marry a young warrior, but they could not malign her in any way. She did not have the normal failings of Mohawk maidens, and she did not invite scandal or gossip.

The date for her baptism was set finally for Easter Sunday, 1676. She had fulfilled all of the required courses and had taken part in the Christian community activities with a generous spirit. Father de Lamberville could deny her no longer, and he set the date and allowed the Christians to decorate the chapel in honor of the occasion. It was important, naturally, and the local Christians well understood the significance of having such a distinguished convert in their midst. As it turned out, the entire Mohawk population had an interest in the ceremony marking the acceptance of the Black-robe religion by a prominent member of the clan. The chapel was again decorated with pine bows, beads, pelts, feathers, ribbons and colorful arrangements of wild flowers.

Father de Lamberville named her Katherine, or Kateri, in honor of St. Catherine of Siena, one that was used frequently for women converts. Many Native Americans bore that name as a result of the work of the Blackrobes, but none would carry it with more spiritual fervor or perfection. When she was baptized, received into the faith and given the name of the famous mystic and saint, Kateri Tekak-witha was only twenty years old.

Kateri Tekakwitha:
The Mystic of the Wilderness

A true flower of the first landscape, the raw and vibrant wilderness of the American Continent, formed by the second massive landscape, the Iriquois Nations and their remarkable traditions and spiritual insights, and welcomed at last into the third, the Catholic Church, the treasure house of Christian truth, Kateri began the last phase of her brief life. Being a convert and receiving the sacraments after so many years of searching and waiting, she was filled with an exaltation that altered her vision of everything around her. The sky was bluer, the rolling hills more alive to the rain, the forest lovelier and more inviting. She was home, free of the constraints that had dominated her interior and exterior lives, and she was at peace, having found her way into the embrace of Holy Mother the Church. To the other Christians she was like a pillar of fire, burning, sparkling, vibrating with the myriad glories of Christ.

All of these reactions are experienced by most converts to Catholicism, whether they distinguish themselves in later years or not. For each the reception of baptism means the expunging of the past, the rapture of having discovered truth amid so many lies, and the joy of becoming part of a universal family, both on earth and in heaven. It is the plunge into the depths of love and the spirit, so far removed from the half-way measures of many human lives. Kateri experienced all of these things as part of the process of conversion, and she was now a part of a community of faith that nourished her and protected her with guidelines for spiritual perfection.

In the days ahead, when she listened to the counsel of her companions or heard of the practices of the saints, Kateri would be led to excesses in penance and in attempting to attain perfection. The excesses stemmed from her generosity of heart, her overwhelming sense of unworthiness and from the fact that she was a rarified soul living in the wilderness. Not everyone in the village or in the mission was capable of recognizing the true horizons of her spirituality, and not everyone was capable of steering her in the right direction. For this reason, Kateri's patience and her untiring efforts to incorporate the various spiritual exercises into her daily life become even more remarkable. The fact that her true vocation was well beyond the understanding of her contemporaries in the wilderness added suffering to her in many ways, but she never turned aside, never complained and attempted to find her way to her own spiritual destiny.

Kateri had entered the fourth landscape of her existence, the domain of the spirit, where union with God assumes a lustrous beauty, an intimacy and a vibrancy that makes everything else in the world pale and fade. Baptism was a specific grace for her soul, but it was also a formalizing of the process which had been taking place deep within her all along. The sacrament welcomed her with an even greater urgency to the Divine Embrace.

Actually, in all things Kateri was imitating her namesake, Catherine of Siena, who was a true mystic and a contemplative. The Church, in canonizing Catherine and others of her nature, declares that there are many ways in which souls can achieve salvation through grace. The various religious congregations and orders within the Church have been established with the same realization in mind, to provide adequate and prudent frameworks upon which men and women can work toward their own perfection according to the promptings of the Holy Spirit.

The Jesuit priests and the other missionaries in the American wilds gave evidence of the "way of light," the active apostolate that is most common to Christians. While on earth, Jesus Christ was very explicit about the ways in which his followers could imitate him: through the practice of the virtues, through good works, and through love. Most human beings who take being Christian seriously make some attempt to lead virtuous and exemplary lives, distinguished by charity, by compassion and by a prudent perception of the world and its mad vanities.

The religious congregations and orders which train men and women for work in the missions, in hospitals, schools, sanitariums, chapels, social services, communications and in countless other institutions which offer the weak or the afflicted genuine care, are based on the Christian concepts of unstinting devotion to Christ and of generosity to Christ's own, the family of mankind. Such a path is difficult, as the demands of caring, of tending to the ill or abused, and all of those activities designed to combat the illusions of the world, exhaust bodies and spirits. Maintaining the Christian spirit of joy amid submission, of kindness in the heat of persecution, charity in the torments of martyrdom, involve the highest faculties of fidelity, honor and courage. Above all, the active apostolate demands an unstinting awareness of the lures of the world and the failings of other human beings. The many saints of the past have given remarkable testimony to the variety of ways in which true sons and daughters of the Church can aid the world. The "way of light" is even present on the earth today, as some of our more distinguished religious confound the world with their own recognizable heroic virtue.

There is another path, however, called the "way of darkness," the one which our Lord meant when he stated that "the Kingdom of God is within you." It is the path of prayer, but not the type of prayer that most men and women experience in their lifetimes. It is the mystical road, the way of love and union. It is the road of contemplation. Contemplation as experienced by people in this spiritual world, can be translated rather simply as meaning "the joyful gaze of the soul upon God."

The use of the word *darkness* in this particular form of spiritual advancement does not indicate evil, shadows, or blindness. The "dark path" is called that because human beings who are called to the mystical life enter a realm of the spirit in which their senses are not reliable guides for them as they move toward their spiritual goals. The missionary, for example, can tell by the reception of the faith how well he is serving Christ and the people. He can number converts, witness changes in behavior, can even count the missions that he establishes in the wilderness. The monks and nuns in the great contemplative monasteries and convents, called by many the Church's "treasuries of grace," support the missionary with their sacrifices, their penances and their prayers. They never see the results personally. They do not admit converts or establish great mission houses in the wilds. Nothing is visible to them, but they persevere, knowing only that they are called to this form of worship and to this manner of bringing graces to mankind.

While some mystics are well known in their day, men and women such as St. John of the Cross and St. Teresa of Avila, many of them work out their own apostolate of praise and prayer quite hidden and unappreciated. When St. Thérèse the Little Flower died, for example, some of her own Carmelite Sisters asked what there was to write about her life. They had lived with her as she endured her own agonies of the spirit, had shared meals and prayers with her as she ascended into the heights of mystical union, but they had not understood what was taking place. The mystical souls of this world most often appear as the gentlest, the most docile, the sweetest of all.

They have just stepped beyond the usual human experience. For instance, every human being on earth desires companionship, fulfillment in love, commitment to the highest degree and union with someone who can be all things to his or her life. Marriage provides considerable companionship, fulfillment, commitment and union, but even in the happiest stages of wedded bliss humans still feel drawn to something well beyond the intimacies of flesh and the visible personality. The spiritual side of men and women yearns for oblation, for the simple act of melting into the Presence of the One. The world, friends, honors, career accomplishments, even loved ones cannot provide what the spiritual nature of human beings seek as the natural domain of the soul.

Contemplatives and mystics, those who are gifted by grace with "the joyful gaze of the soul upon God," by instinct are drawn to move beyond the flesh and the realm of the senses. They have a different vision about the world, a rather special understanding. Someone once said that a contemplative is able to rise above the world to see it in its entirety and in its finished form. It is like a person looking down upon an exquisite coverlet. From below, the stitches, the mistakes, the knots of fabric and threads are all exposed. The work is complete but it is not so grand from this angle. From above, however, where the master craftsman has created a pattern of vibrancy and color, of flowing form and style, the coverlet assumes a fascinating identity of its own, imprinted with beauty and charm. The contemplatives of this world, the mystics, see the completed pattern or at least understand the manner in which God is moving and forming all things for the good of souls, no longer caring about mistakes, knotted fabrics or threads.

This awareness is centered in the recognition of the Presence of God, a spiritual insight that has long been the foundation for many saintly careers. Such a recognition, naturally, alters the contemplative's perception of the world and the individual. Each event, each person's honors, sufferings and death become blended in the pattern which God has allowed, and living within the framework of such a unified whole gives the mystic a unique vision about temporal affairs. At the same time, coming closer to God, the mystics normally develop an acute consciousness of unworthiness, of true wretchedness when compared with the Divine. For this reason mystics are given to great penances, to a life concerned with merit, sacrifice, atonement and reparation. The great contemplative religious communities which provide a monastic setting for the perfecting of human souls, have long been considered harsh and austere. The religious within their walls have taken upon themselves strict diets, limited conversations, simple clothing, labors, prayers and reparations. Not afraid to be alone with The Alone, these religious pursue their vocations in giving praise, in repenting for themselves and others, and in moving toward the loss of self in the embrace of the Divine. Outsiders who are privileged to visit such monasteries and convents, however, discover that these "austere" religious are normally cheerful, charming, humorous and balanced in the performance of their daily routines. They display the "sweet docility" which Kateri made evident always.

Long before baptism and acceptance into the Catholic community, Kateri Tekakwitha had discerned the Presence of God in her life. She needed no monastic structure to make this evident. She needed no counsel in order to recognize the embrace of The Alone. Her conversion only deepened her spirit and allowed the flowering of true graces in her soul. Had she been in a convent, behind the walls and instructed by the religious who were trained in the mystical life, she would have matured as rapidly, but her role would have been altered. She was the Lily of the Mohawks, the Mystic of the Wilderness, and it was her destiny to attain her spiritual heights in the dense forests of the land.

Immediately after her baptism, of course, the floodgates of her soul opened, and she began to seek more and more solitude and to take on extended periods of prayer. The union with the One had begun, and she was experiencing a rapturous encounter at last. This did not make her particularly popular in the village, naturally. Perhaps her uncle and her other relatives had hoped that by becoming a Christian she would settle some problem within her and would become more involved in village life. They had no way of knowing that more and more she was shocked by what she saw around her, saddened by the brutality and the paganism and alienated by the mindless pursuit of the flesh. The people of the village had not suddenly turned into mad animals. The very ones who had cared for her over the years had not become barbaric savages, but their concerns about daily life, their interest in the flesh and in pleasures made them strangers to Kateri as she became more and more involved in prayer. She had never liked the celebration of the yearly festivals, finding them pagan and cruel.

The act of drawing apart from her own community marked Kateri as an enemy in the minds of most. Her Mohawk contemporaries, especially the young people with whom she was expected to associate, took her isolation as a form of rebuke. She was setting herself up as a special person in their eyes, drawing attention to her conversion and alienating everyone else. These contemporaries, typical of the young in almost every culture, could not allow her to continue in her ways without registering their annoyance and their resentment. In some accounts of Kateri's life these young people are portrayed as cruel devils. It is far more likely that the young men and women were simply acting on their innate sense of conformity. They wanted Kateri to join in their activities, to be part of their generation, and to accept their particular outlooks and ideals. When she stood apart from them, they responded the way many young people the world over would respond, with anger, intolerance and cruelty. It was not because they were urged by their paganism or by devilish hatred. These young Mohawk men and women were blind to her spirituality, ignorant of the realm in which she dwelt, and utterly mindless of her needs as an individual.

Kateri no longer attended the tribal festivals or gatherings, working alone always and entering the woods to pray whenever she could get away. She especially refrained from all of her normal activities on Sundays and holy days, something that the Mohawks did not understand at all. By doing this, she naturally brought down upon herself the complaint that since converting she no longer had an interest in performing her chores satisfactorily. She worked extra hours before and after each Sunday or holy day, but that did not matter and was not counted by her family and neighbors. All they knew was that when she was needed she was not there.

The Mohawk young people and even some elders began to laugh at her, to taunt her, even to make obscene gestures when she passed. They were particularly annoyed by the fact that Kateri was becoming very devoted to the recitation of the rosary and kept one in her hand whenever possible. She had started learning about the Blessed Virgin Mary and about this most efficacious form of prayer. The Rosary symbolized many spiritual concepts for her, and its readiness, at hand, consoled her as she kept to her daily routines in a totally pagan atmosphere. Even Kateri's relatives told her to put the rosary away, and, docile as usual, she probably kept it close but hidden when in their company.

Her growing devotion to the Blessed Virgin Mary increased, however, when she was allowed to go with a group of Christians to Tionnontoguen, the Mohawk capital, some distance from her village. There a rather unique and fabled statue was being installed on the Feast of the Immaculate Conception, December 8, 1676. The statue was a replica of one discovered in the trunk of an ancient oak tree in Durant, Belgium, several years before. Depicting the Blessed Mother with the Christ Child in her arms, the statue was exquisite and became the object of pious devotion. Carvers took the wood of the ancient oak and fashioned replicas of the statue from it, sending them to other places. One of these was even sent by boat to New France, given at last to the Mohawk mission.

Kateri was present when the statue was installed at Tionnontoguen, and this wondrous event not only added to her fervor but offered her a more profound realization of the role of the Mother of Christ and the virtue of virginity. What she had chosen in the past as an almost intuitive preference — solitude over marriage, the saving of herself for some great union — became solidly based on Church tradition as a valid lifestyle for her even in the wilderness. She would remain unmarried and alone, thus free to mature in the spiritual life. This statue of the Blessed Virgin depicted once again the attainment of true union with God, and in the arms of the Virgin the Christ Child once again beckoned to Kateri.

When she returned to her village, probably quite enrapt and certainly intrigued by all that she had seen and heard, her persecution increased, reaching the point of actual peril in time. A young warrior, perhaps the one that she had rejected as a young girl, caught Kateri in the forest and told her that if she did not relent her Christian ways he intended to kill her. She is reported to have stayed calm, detached from the violence and therefore more vulnerable. Such an attitude would have brought considerable consternation to the young man, and in the end it would have earned his respect. He fled from the sight of her, leaving behind only his threats. Kateri went on about her business, relating the incident, however, to Father de Lamberville, who was becoming increasingly worried about the situation. Kateri was no longer called Tekakwitha by the villagers. She was simply and rudely known as the "Christian." Even the toddlers laughed at her as she walked on her rounds or performed her chores.

The annual Spring hunting expedition of 1677 proved a turning point for Kateri, as it alarmed De Lamberville and added to his frustrations. He could not protect Kateri from the villagers. He could not even defend her name, because she was mantled by the ways of her family, forced to reside at close quarters with them, and was immersed in the traditions and the routines of their lifestyle. De Lamberville wanted to help Kateri escape, if possible, knowing that the Christian atmosphere of the Sault Mission would not only offer her a physical haven but would hasten her spiritual growth. She had always been frail, given to physical weakness, and he had no idea of how much more persecution she could take without showing the physical and nervous strain. Persecution of the nature that Kateri endured is particularly insidious. It is not a violent attack, which the individual can fend off with a rush of adrenalin or with the overwhelming need for survival. The daily teasing, mocking, laughter and cruel insults were like a chain being forged around her and her activities. Each link was small, vicious and draining, and the priest recognized the signs of exhaustion in her. He marveled that she could conduct herself with such steadfastness, holding to her ideals and marching steadily toward perfection.

If he had misgivings about Kateri's participation in the Spring hunting expedition, De Lamberville could not manage to have her remain alone in the village. She joined her family in the traditional move to the woods and the open fields, as the Mohawks and other members of the Five Nations had always done over the centuries. Certain months out of each year were set aside for a return to the more rustic encampments in the wilderness. Whereas the Mohawks and other Confederate nations were basically town dwellers, these days spent in the wilds not only provided the game that would be needed but offered the men and women a sort of holiday. They chose areas where the game was plentiful, and most campsites were erected on beautiful hills overlooking streams and rivers. The change of scenery was invigorating for a start, and the routines, quite different from those of the towns, allowed the people to relax and to share in many community activities. The Woodland Warriors disappeared for days on end, returning with carcasses on their shoulders. The women maintained their normal household routines and treated the game brought in, but they were also able to enjoy the woods and to be in one another's company. For Kateri the expedition proved to be a special time of prayer. She was able to shelter in secluded areas, free from the taunters and the threats. The loveliness of the surroundings also strengthened her and brought her closer to God.

She spent time with her family, naturally, and during one particular gathering she made an error in addressing her uncle, not using the prescribed formal term of respect. At least this is the account given in records about the source of accusation which developed in time. An aunt, not identified, apparently heard the young maiden address her uncle in a manner which would indicate a close familiarity between them. Obviously the aunt had spent a considerable amount of time watching and waiting for such a sign. She listened, heard what she believed to be an overly familiar tone, and then came to the rather startling conclusion that Kateri and her uncle were involved in a dreaded incestuous relationship. Such a relationship was forbidden by the Five Nations, as it is generally considered evil among all cultures in the world, whether primitive or sophisticated.

As hateful as her conclusions were, the aunt had sense enough not to make her beliefs public. To begin with, Kateri's uncle would have beaten her senseless for bringing such a charge. The aunt kept quiet throughout the expedition, but she made Kateri as miserable as possible in the guise of warning the maiden that she knew about the relationship and would punish her. The aunt did say later that she tried to warn the girl. When the Mohawks returned to the mission, the aunt went immediately to Father de Lamberville to lay before him the ugly truth about his precious convert. She laughed with scorn about the "Christian" who had fooled them all. An incestuous relationship would explain Kateri's refusal to marry, after all, as it would explain her uncle's willingness to allow the maiden to stand against the wishes of the matriarchs. The aunt obviously had a two-fold mission when she spoke to the priest. She wanted to blacken Kateri's name and she wanted to make the priest's work a total mockery.

De Lamberville, a veteran missionary, asked the aunt what proof she could provide other than a single phrase. She admitted that she had nothing else. He then scolded her for slander, gossip and evil thoughts, knowing full well that at the founding of the Five Nations such social ills were condemned in the covenants. The aunt was silenced, and it is not known if she ever mentioned the accusation to anyone else. Father de Lamberville spoke to Kateri as well, informing her of the dreadful charge. She was surprised, but the accusation probably answered questions which she had formed concerning her aunt's attitude and increased hostility. She spoke to the priest about the trials of Christ, as her catechetical instruction had trained her in the Passion of Jesus, and she said that in comparison with what our Lord had suffered she was being exposed to a series of minor inconveniences. Kateri also said that such a relationship was quite impossible for her, thus having no guilt, she had no worries about aunts and their malicious ways.

These considerations evidenced maturity in the face of ugliness and rather sordid imaginings. The words of antagonism were bad enough, but as Father de Lamberville realized, they only laid bare the layers of resentment and intolerance being directed against her. The aunt was only demonstrating the frustration and the rage of the villagers. Kateri had risen above them in many ways, had isolated herself in a spirituality which they could not comprehend, and in so doing invited their attacks. It was becoming increasingly obvious to De Lamberville that her conversion would never be accepted like those of other tribal members. She had always been special, had always carried rank and powers, and her alien manner struck a chord deep within the people, earning their enmity.

De Lamberville could only suggest that Kateri pray before the Blessed Sacrament, not to seek freedom from such suffering but to discover the path that God intended to open before her for her release. He recognized the threats veiled in the accusations. He knew of the young warrior's attack, and he also had an awareness of the nature of the Mohawks when they were crossed or threatened. Kateri would die at their hands without complaint, probably rejoicing that she had been deemed worthy enough to suffer such an end for the faith. The people, however, if driven to such a crime, would bring down upon themselves a dreadful condition. De Lamberville began to implore heaven for a solution.

The answer to their prayers arrived soon after in the person of an Oneida chief named Okenratariken (Garonhiague), also known to the French as *Cendre Chaude* or *Poudre Chaud*, which is translated as "Hot Cinders" or as "Hot Powder." Those colorful images were chosen by the French because they represented the temper of the man. He was what is known as a "short-fused" individual who could fly off the handle into a rage at the slightest provocation. Powerful, strong and relentless, Hot Cinders was a man to be reckoned with, and the early French learned to walk carefully when in his company. The Iroquois also honored Hot Cinders as a man who was brave, resolute and honorable.

Several years before his arrival at Gandawague, Hot Cinders was hunting when a friend brought word of his brother's death. He blamed the French, naturally, and he started out for the city of Montreal, then called Ville Marie, where he intended to hunt down the murderers and take his vengeance upon them. On the way, however, Hot Cinders was informed that his brother had not been slain by the French but by another party altogether. He listened to the details of the murder, thought about the situation and then continued on to Montreal in order to maintain the safety of his people. Hot Cinders had sworn revenge upon the murderers, and if he returned to the Oneida nation, the other chiefs and warriors would be obliged to aid him in his vengeance. War would erupt within the Five Nations, and many good people would die in order to satisfy his honor. Being a chief of the Oneidas, trained in the ways of the nations and in the ramifications of one man's desires, Hot Cinders knew that he could not bring his people into his private affairs.

He remained in Montreal for the same reason, and in time he was joined by his wife, a woman named Marie Garhi. These two had a most remarkable marriage. They had been espoused according to Iroquois traditions at the tender age of eight. They had started living together then, as brother and sister, and they had never separated. In time the union was made whole and complete, and the pair remained constant and close over the years, as the result of their growing up together and their sharing of all that life offered them.

Hot Cinders, however, was not the same man that he had been when he started out on the path of vengeance. During his stay in Montreal he had been in the company of many that he respected, and in the process he had discovered the fact that they were now Christians. Learning as much as he could about a religion that could turn his friends into gentle, kindly and compassionate beings, Hot Cinders decided to accept catechetical instructions. The missionaries in Montreal also practiced the custom of making converts of adult age take weekly classes and prove themselves worthy of baptism. Hot Cinders, naturally, brought all the force of his personality into his conversion, honing his honor, his courage and his mental prowess in the changes taking place. When baptised he was given the name Louis, after Saint Louis, King of France, that gentle and ascetic ruler, and he became an exemplary member of the Christian community.

He attended two Masses a day, received Holy Communion, was especially devoted to the Blessed Sacrament and conducted all of his affairs with calm. Word of his conversion, naturally, spread across Iroquoia, and his former warrior companions made the long trek to Montreal to discover for themselves what had taken place. They were quite stunned to find Hot Cinders spreading the doctrines of Christianity, but they listened attentively, drawn as usual by his fiery eloquence.

It is difficult for modern Catholics to understand the remarkable impact that the faith had upon the Iroquois nation and its leaders. Certainly the ideals and spiritual concepts of these Native Americans prepared them for the profoundly beautiful aspects of Christianity, and their sense of obligation and honor fitted them admirably for the tasks of carrying out the commands of Christ throughout their lives. They came to the Church with a unified purpose, with strength tested in the wilderness, and with a basic wisdom about the earth and mankind that fortified their beliefs. Certainly not every Iroquois was a magnificent specimen of the faith, as that does not happen in any land, but the early converts were great enough to cause a sensation among their own people.

After discussing the situation, the Oneida elders went to Hot Cinders and asked him to return as their chief again. He could practice his faith, instruct others and fulfill whatever he believed to be his destiny as a Christian. The former chief, however, recognized the dangers of his returning to the wilderness and set about making a series of proposals that he knew his own would not be able to accept in good faith. First he demanded that all of the Oneidas in his tribe become Christians. That was very difficult for them, because not all of them had been convinced of the need to put aside their traditional spirituality. Even more of them might have considered making a conversion, but the Church represented not only Christ and the Saints but the white men, particularly the French. They balked at this but did not actually refuse to accept the first condition. Hot Cinders, therefore, made his second demand, which he knew would put an end to all negotiations about his return. He insisted that the Oneidas abandon their tribal lands and live in the Sault Mission. This was impossible, and he knew that as well as they did. The Oneidas would never give up their ancestral sites, not even for Hot Cinders and his new faith. Such a move would not only put them at the mercy of the white men but would allow others to intrude and slowly engulf the lands of the People of the Stone, the *O-na-yoté-ka*. The elders sadly bade Hot Cinders goodbye and went away, wondering what sort of power had overtaken their leader. Hot Cinders, resolved, maintained his Christian ways and led a very distinguished life, becoming chief of Sault Mission in time. He was slain in 1684 in a war with the Senecas.

In Kateri's time, however, Hot Cinders not only administered Indian affairs at Sault Mission but went on journeys throughout the Iroquois territories, accompanied by trusted friends. He and Kryn, the "Great Mohawk" visited the various villages of Iroquoia to talk to their people about the faith. Eloquent orators, the two men spent days on the trails, stopping to gather the members of the

Five Nations so that they could explain their conversion and the beauty of the Church in their lives. The two famed leaders, naturally, reached far more Indians than the missionaries could, and they were able to explain the Catholic faith in terms that were far more reasonable and enticing.

In 1677, Hot Cinders, accompanied by a Huron from the Mission of Lorette and by a relative of Kateri, arrived in Gandawague to speak to the Catholic converts and to address the villagers. This maternal relative has been reported in some accounts as the brother-in-law of Kateri Tekakwitha, married to her half sister. In some versions of Kateri's life, her uncle adopted a second daughter. Nothing is known of her life as a child, however, and the woman is only casually identified as Kateri's half sister later in her biography.

The relative, the Huron Christian and Hot Cinders came with the usual tapestry, the beautifully colored illustration of Christian life, serving as a *Do giquese*, a catechist, to the people. When the tapestry was raised up in a village, the people came to listen to the talks and to ponder the power of the faith that could attract such eloquent and gifted veterans of life. Kateri listened to their words, and in her heart she knew that they had been sent to Gandawague as her release. She knew that the men were stopping over just for a few days. When they left, she intended to accompany them, going to Sault Mission, which Hot Cinders described as a garden of eden for converts.

Father de Lamberville, as sorry as he was to see her go from his charge, agreed with Kateri and advised her to talk to the men and to make arrangements. He then sat down at his desk and wrote a letter to the priests of Sault Mission, one that he knew would alert them to Kateri's special needs and potential. Haste was the primary factor, as Kateri's uncle was not in the village at the time. Kateri's aunts, apparently, did not raise any commotion about her leaving. Certainly these women, aware of everything that went on in the village, would have seen her making preparations for the trip.

When the men believed that they had done as much as possible for the people there, Hot Cinders and his companions went to their canoes. The chief intended to push on to his own lands in the Oneida territories in order to make a visit to his own people and to continue his catechetical activities. For this reason he placed Kateri in the keeping of his two companions, knowing them to be honorable men. One was even related to Kateri, and he would safeguard her in the wilds.

The three set off in one canoe, as Hot Cinders paddled in the opposite direction. Just how many of the people in the village saw them leave is not known, but the cry went up a short time later when it was discovered that Kateri was gone, and the three men were gone with her. A discussion was held in Gandawague and then a runner was sent with the dire news to Kateri's uncle, who was visiting the white men at a nearby fort. The uncle, furious at what he believed was a kidnapping or a planned escape, hurried back to the village and took up his gun, filling it with three bullets, as if he expected to slay all three of the men before dragging Kateri back to his longhouse. He must have given Father de Lamberville a very difficult time as well, blaming him for the loss of his niece and adopted daughter.

Meanwhile, the fugitives, having paddled some distance, had split up temporarily, as the Huron made his way to the Dutch settlements, hoping to beg some bread there. This lack of supplies indicates that the departure from Gandawague was hurried and in secret. The Huron directed his canoe toward the Dutch and found himself in the path of Kateri's uncle, who was paddling furiously in search of the escapees. As the uncle did not know the Huron by sight, being away from the village during the man's brief stay there, he passed him without a word. The Huron, however, doubled back quickly and alerted Kateri and her relative. They moved away from the river, knowing that the uncle was a superb tracker and paddler. The Huron fell back as a rear guard, knowing that the uncle would soon be visible on the horizon. Kateri and her relative raced through the forest trails, seeking shelter and trying to put some ground between them and the stalking war chief of Gandawague.

The uncle did appear on the horizon, as the Huron had expected, and he fired a shot into the air to warn the others and then set about beating the bushes as if looking for game. Again the uncle was unaware of the identity of the man. He did not even recognize him as the man he had seen on the river. The uncle raced past the rear guard and plunged into the woods, where he came across another Indian, sitting calmly by the side of the trail, smoking. This was Kateri's relative, who had hidden her carefully and then had staked out a position that was quite obvious and therefore deceptive. The uncle had never laid eyes on this man before either, so he stalked off, still looking for his prey. He continued his hunt for several hours, covering vast tracts of land, but then he gave in to his frustrations and made his way back to Gandawague, knowing that Kateri was lost to the village forever.

This uncle, identified as Iowerano in one source, is a pivotal figure in the early life of Kateri Tekakwitha, but remains somewhat of an enigma, shrouded in his duties and in his command position in the clans. Certainly he was a man of considerable compassion and concern, as evidenced by his adoption of Kateri and perhaps of a second daughter. He also showed that he honored his brother's memory in this act, but the care of orphans and others weakened or made vulnerable by tragedy was an Iroquois hallmark, at least within the confines of their own populations. They showed no such mercy to outsiders who fell as victims into their hands. Then, of course, their fates were sealed by the matriarchs, and their deaths, hideous and prolonged, came at feminine hands. Iowerano, in his anger over the flight of Kateri, was probably prompted by several motives, the loss of his prestige being paramount. He was a chief, used to being obeyed by those under his command, and certainly this maiden had defied him over the decades. He also sought her out of affection as well, determined to drag her back and to make her conform to the Mohawk traditional roles, if for no other reason than to insure her safety and her ultimate happiness. As it was, he disappears from the scene forever, and nothing is known of his activities after that last dreadful hunt through the forests.

The fugitives, the three Christians who were bent on seeing Kateri safe and sound at Sault Mission, managed to elude the stalker and began their journey in earnest. They probably carried their canoe to the Hudson River, where they could paddle up to Jessup's Landing, crossing then to Luzerne in the north and on to Lake George, then called Lake St. Sacrament. There the canoe which had been hidden carefully by Hot Cinders at the start of the journey, was used by the three to cross into Lake Champlain. From there the route led to the Richelieu River, where Kateri reached Sault Mission in the autumn of 1677. She had retraced the steps of her Christian mother, who had been taken from the mission into the wilds, captured and then dragged into the Mohawk realms. Kateri said later that her joy increased with each mile that they covered in the wilderness. Certainly her companions, tried and tested Christians, must have seemed like angels to her, as they carried on the daily prayer rituals ingrained in them by their catechetical training and by their lifestyles in the Christian missions. Although they moved through the rugged wilderness, which was dangerous because of hostile tribes and animals, they kept the spirit of Christ alive in their hearts. Kateri was entering a paradise of sorts, a site devoted to all of the spiritual ideals which had taken hold of her heart and soul. She did not anticipate being free of suffering there, as she was wise already in the way of the Holy Cross, but at least she could serve the Church and Christ without being terrorized by her family and neighbors.

She carried with her a letter from Father de Lamberville, directed to the pastors of the mission, Father Fremin, and his assistants, Father Cholonec, who was a Jesuit from Brittany, a devoted, amiable man. A Father Chauchetiere is also mentioned in the records. The letter introduced Kateri to these priests, and in it Father de Lamberville advised them: "I send you a treasure, guard it well."

The mission which welcomed Kateri and her companions at the end of their long and arduous journey, had originally been built at the southern end of La Prairie. That site had been recognized almost immediately as being ill advised. The soil in the region was bad, discouraging the farming occupations of the converts and making their food rations short. At the same time, the mission was too close to the various French settlements. This proximity involved the Christian Native Americans in French affairs, which benefited them by introducing them to European ways but also made them subject to the bigotry, intolerance and general cantankerousness of the local French settlers. The Jesuit priests normally maintained a distance from their own kind in establishing their missions, isolating the new converts to a degree in order to shelter them and to prevent unnecessary interference from the seculars, the average lay men and women of the colonies.

The King of France, the resplendent Louis XIV, solved the problem by granting a new territory to the Jesuits on April 29, 1680. He provided them with a site at Sault near La Prairie of de Madeleine. This was positioned three to four miles up river from La Prairie, where the Portage River emptied into the mighty St. Lawrence. On a wide plateau, which resulted from the joining of these two waterways, the mission was ideally situated, both from a scenic and a fortification standpoint. In front of the complex was the beautiful Lake St. Paul, and in the distance were Ville-Marie (Montreal) and Mount Royal. On the left was the exquisite Heron Island, surrounded by azure water, standing isolated and lovely against the horizon at the foot of the rapids. The mission was called St. Francis Xavier of Sault St. Louis as a result. *Sault* translates from the French as rapids.

The rather peculiar thinking involved in the land grant by King Louis XIV, of course, did not strike any of the priests or the French court. He was giving away land without a single recognition of its present or previous owners. It was assumed by the white men that the king possessed all of the lands in that part of North America, and therefore he was merely exercising his royal rights in order to provide the Jesuits with a needed site. The fact that the land was already occupied — and had been for centuries — by Native American tribes, had no connection or impact upon the white man's acquisition and distribution of land tracts in the "wilderness" of the New World. As Spain acted in the southern regions of the continent, so France, England and the Dutch accumulated land areas and used them as they saw fit. No one discussed the moral or legal ramifications of such possession or use. The Native Americans were mere spectators in the division of North America, as their counterparts were massacred and enslaved for their holdings in Mesoamerica and in the realm of the Incas.

The actual mission of St. Francis Xavier of Sault St. Louis was composed of a chapel and adjoining work areas and residences for the priests stationed there. The entire complex was surrounded by a rather stout stockade, in case of attack, and the cabins of the Christian Native Americans were built outside of these defensive walls. There was an advantage to this sort of building actually. The Spanish brought all of their converts inside the main walls of the missions, most of which were rather large and commanding. The Native Americans were thus brought into contact with European customs by force, and they were allowed to govern themselves only to a point. The French priests preferred to allow the Native Americans to conduct their own affairs entirely, providing only a sheltering spiritual haven. In case of attack, these converts could come within the walls for defensive purposes.

Standing on a rise, surrounded by forests, streams, Lake Paul and the splendor of the countryside, Sault Mission's Indian population numbered approximately 120 to 150, and they resided in sixty cabins. Their lives were much like the ones they had led in their home villages, with the usual farm labors, gathering in the fields, hunting, and household chores. The Indians moved into wilderness campsites during the year to conduct the annual hunting expeditions, which provided game for their larders and allowed them to be free of all restraints imposed by the presence of the Europeans.

The setting of the mission, the wilderness which the Indians knew and reverenced as part of the divine plan for all humans, combined in a natural and gentle manner to offer the converts of the faith a perfect and isolated stage upon which their spiritual development continued without interruption. With men like Kryn and Hot Cinders available to them, urging them forward and enforcing the Christian doctrines, the people were able to exist as a rare Christian community in the wilds. Hot Cinders spoke to them eloquently of Christ, of the barbaric nature of their past existences, and of the joys awaiting each soul that clung to Christ and his Cross.

The piety which resulted, and the unstinting manner in which the Christian Indians lived in commune, astounded the white men and women who came into contact with them. Rumors about Sault Mission spread throughout New France, and many came to visit the chapel, to speak to the priests and even to participate in the religious services. They left edified and stunned by the example which the Indians set for the rest of humanity. Alerted to the conditions at the mission, Bishop de St. Vallier of Ville Marie (Montreal), also went to see conditions for himself. He had believed the rumors about the piety and spirituality to be quaint and rather exaggerated, but his short stay among the Iroquois taught him that they had ascended to another level of Christian participation, and he reported that everything said of these converts was true. In time, the local French attended services at the mission chapel, not to sit and gape at the converts but to be replenished and revitalized in grace and in the faith. The Indians, tolerant as always, allowed such white men and women access to their devotions.

All was calm, all was still and serene. The only sounds that echoed through the area were those of Indian families at their daily labors, interspersed with the great tolling sound of the mission bell which set the schedule for religious services and for prayers. Even the Angelus was rung on that bell, echoing out across the fields and the forests. The Christian Indians halted their labors throughout the mission area when the Angelus was tolled, and they recited the lovely greeting to Our Lady, echoing in the New World the same prayers being said in countless communities across the earth. They were one with the white men, not in progress, not in civilizing efforts, but in the true vocation of all human beings, in the affairs of the spirit.

One of the most remarkable aspects of Sault Mission, actually, was its diverse population. Tribal members that held enmity or hostility throughout the decades were living side by side there. The very tribes that had warred on one another in the past now laid aside their rivalries and feuds in the name of Christ. Using the strengths of the Indian people as a whole — the sense of honor, the courage, generosity and daring — the converts bound themselves as one in the name of Catholicism. They were the bearers of Christ's light in the wilderness, and as such they conducted themselves with kindness, humility and incredible fortitude.

When Kateri arrived in this haven, it was decided that she would live with her relatives, in the company of the man who had escorted her from her village, and with his wife. There are references that this woman was Kateri's "sister," but she certainly was not related to her in any physical sense. This could have been the second daughter adopted by the war chief, a woman who had married and had followed her husband to the mission. Such a view poses a severe and obvious problem, of course. Kateri's uncle would certainly have recognized a son-in-law on the trail in the forest. He is depicted in the accounts as passing him by, thinking him to be just another Indian smoking while taking a brief rest in his hunting quest. The man was probably related to Kateri on her mother's side, a stranger to Iowerano and the other Mohawks of the village.

In any case, Kateri moved into their cabin and was welcomed warmly, discovering as well an older woman named Anastasia, who shared the residence. Anastasia had been a close friend of Kateri's mother before she was captured and taken into the Mohawk lands. She opened her arms and her heart to Kateri and delighted in discovering the child of her past companion.

Within the house and in the fields, Kateri set about earning her place in the community, showing the same willingness and fidelity that had distinguished her even in the times of persecution among her own. She was coming to life, stunned by the beauty of the mission site and by the almost angelic atmosphere of the city. All of the graces and spiritual ideals which had blossomed unseen for so many years began to blossom at the Sault.

The life of the mission was certainly conducive to her spiritual development. The Jesuits maintained a strict control over the religious services and practices, never allowing themselves to slack or lessen their obligations. Each day started at 4:00 a.m., as the last stars were fading in the night sky and the forests lay mantled by the mists and the chill of the early hours. In that stillness, in that moment of hushed beauty, the priests rose to recite the Divine Office, the Breviary, as it was being recited in monasteries and convents throughout Europe. This recitation not only confirmed the religious vocations of the priests but united them in spirit with the Church in the world. The mission bell was rung at that hour, alerting the local Indian Christians, who rose and made their way to the chapel or began their private devotions in their cabins.

Two Masses were celebrated each morning, the first by the priests after recitation of the Divine Office, and another at 8:00 a.m., attended by the congregation. Many of the locals, however, rose and made their way to the first Mass as well. Kateri learned quickly that the Mass was open to her, and she began her day with the first bell. These Masses were quite unique, in that they were accompanied by chants in the Iroquois language, sometimes in full harmony, as in the festivals of the Mohawk and other villages of the Five Nations. Again the wilderness resounded with such harmony, as human voices were raised to greet the first lights of each day and to give praise. The sermons of the Masses were often preached by Iroquois leaders as well. Their eloquence stirred the congregation and urged them to greater spiritual perfection. A rosary often followed the Masses, and the people returned throughout the day to meditate and pray before the Blessed Sacrament in the chapel.

Kateri attended the Mass at dawn and then remained in prayer until the city Mass at 8:00 a.m., which was preceded by the Sacrament of Confession. During this second Mass the men sat on one side, and the women on the other. There was also a special group of converts, members of the Brotherhood of the Holy Family. This was a rather unique pious association, devised by the Jesuits to honor the more advanced among their converts and to bring a stabilizing, spiritually oriented continuity to the mission congregations. Only the finest among the converts were admitted to this association, and they took their responsibilities and their honors seriously. The Brotherhood served as a counterpart to the traditional Keepers of the Faith in many ways, maintaining the moral tone of the congregation and exercising wisdom in Indian affairs. The freedom that the Native American communities had in the Jesuit missions again hastened the independent efforts of the individuals and allowed each man and woman to advance spiritually. This is not to say that each person in the Iroquois Christian communities reflected the highest virtues or epitomized the saintly. Most human beings, whether Native American, white or otherwise, do not aspire to the same levels of spiritual growth. Some are born with limited capacities for learning, for self-rule, for personal development. Some are gifted but not prone to exercising the sort of heroic efforts necessary. The same variations were visible at Sault Mission, but the distinguishing hallmark of the congregation living there is the effort made by one and all to achieve a peaceful, grace-stimulating world in which young persons like Kateri could flower easily. This, naturally, reflects once again the great vision, the Tree of Peace, the founding of the Five Nations, where men and women living in the wilds of the New World banded together to bring harmony, cooperation and peace to their domains.

The Brotherhood of the Holy Family, as a pious association, met each day at 1:00 p.m., where the members recited prayers and discussed mission affairs. At 3:00 p.m., the entire congregation joined the Brotherhood at Vespers, the beautiful Divine Office which not only closes the liturgical themes of each day but anticipates the festival to be celebrated on the morrow. At Vespers, the congregation chanted psalms which Father Fremin had translated into Iroquois, using the monastic tones. The service normally ended with Benediction of the Blessed Sacrament.

Kateri's devotions, and those of the more pious Christians of Sault, did not revolve solely around the scheduled religious services in the chapel. Even the local landscape offered the wise places of meditation and contemplation. On the banks of the river a gigantic cross had been raised as a symbol of the hallowed site and the intention of the local populace. Unrestrained by the forces which had made her life so difficult in her village, Kateri used the chapel services and the natural loveliness of the surroundings to practice all of the Christian ideals which had formed in her heart in secret for so many years. She also listened, watched and imitated the calm, serene and highly devoted individuals in the mission. Father Cholonec described her in the early days, saying that she almost burst with happiness in being in such an atmosphere of prayer and grace. He added:

> Her soul was well disposed toward perfection; and throwing herself into this with singular devotion, she adopted all the practices which she saw were good. . . It was only a matter of a

few weeks until she stood out among all the other women and girls of the mission . . . in a short time, a saint among the just and faithful.

Retiring as always, normally keeping her head covered with a shawl, Kateri chose the companionship of Anastasia, which was a normal reaction. This woman was not only wise in the ways of the mission and the Christian life, but she was a link to Kateri's past. Anastasia could sit for hours talking about Kateri's mother and about the saints. The older woman slowly introduced her to the practices held in common in the mission, but she offered her advice on appearance, demeanor and attitudes as well. For example, Kateri arrived wearing elaborate hair decorations, and Anastasia encouraged her to shed them as vanities.

Also, the attitude of most of the Christian Indians was one of remorse and repentance, particularly among those who had converted late in life. Such remorse for the past was the result of their recognition of grace, of unique opportunities, and of the rather hideous customs which they had practiced before their conversions. Many had taken part in the village festivals, in the barbaric cruelty to war prisoners and slaves, and perhaps even in the ritualized slaying of the enemy. Men and women had shared in atrocities, as they had participated in drunken sprees and in immoral relationships. They looked back on such things with horror and with sorrow, particularly as the faith introduced them to the beautiful ways of Christ and to the spiritualizing of existence.

Kateri, seeing this genuine remorse and listening to the grief which the converts exhibited, followed their lead and repented her own past. The fact that she had never allowed herself to take part in the barbaric traditions of her own people, customs which she instinctively understood as destructive to her soul, did not occur to her. She knew that she had never violated herself physically, had never indulged in drink or in the festival antics. She knew that she was blameless of any murders or tortures. Such innocence, however, did not spare her from remorse over the years wasted without the sacraments, years lost to her in the midst of paganism and persecution.

Imitating the others, Kateri began a series of physical punishments, using switches to beat her back and shoulders, walking barefoot in the snow, staying awake throughout the nights in prayer and limiting herself to one meal of porridge each day. Such excesses were part of the atonement process of others. Kateri, who had never indulged in the same sinful activities as a child or as a young woman, performed them out of recognition of her own failings, and out of love.

This binding power of love became the center of her existence, in fact, rooted in her practice of the Presence of God. As a mystic, she was acutely aware of the Most Blessed Trinity, the Father, Son and Holy Spirit, and she understood the simple vocation of each human being on earth — giving praise to the Most High. In this manner, Kateri reflected her patron saint, Catherine of Siena, and the other contemplatives of the past. She remained constant in demonstrating her awareness of the Presence of God, using this awareness to spiritualize and perfect even the simplest of tasks. The Little Flower and other great saints of the past performed all of their daily routines in the same spirit, thus raising them above the mundane and the common and earning graces for themselves and their contemporaries.

While it is difficult for moderns to understand the lengths to which such mystics went in offering God their lives, their talents and their souls, the love which they felt within them compelled them to make sacrifices and to endure all things. Kateri loved God, gazed upon him with joy. She was being led to the understanding of the true role of the soul in giving praise, in imitating the Choirs of Angels that surround the Throne of God with hymns and chants. Like all mystics before her, she was entering the landscape of praise, of worship, of unstinting devotion to the Beloved. Kateri was becoming more and more alone with The Alone, in the wilderness, in the chapel, even in the company of her fellow mission converts. This was the crux of her life at Sault. She listened to the advice of people like Anastasia, sought to imitate the tried and true practices of those who repented the past, but she was blameless, innocent, pure as the radiant lily. If she involved herself in excesses, it was not because she sought to distinguish herself in the mission or to court the praise of others. Kateri was a child in the faith, untutored in the more profound areas of mortification and penance. No one needed to teach her prayer or contemplation, as the Bridegroom had sought her out in the wilderness.

Despite her efforts to remain hidden, Kateri's reputation grew rapidly, and the priests began to understand the ramifications of Father de Lamberville's letter to them. As a sign of their appreciation of her spirituality, it was announced that Kateri would receive Holy Communion at Christmas. She had not yet been allowed to make her First Communion. This was part of the Jesuit approach to conversions, one that extended into all areas of their training. The converts were taught to understand the true essence of the sacraments, and they were allowed to approach them only after demonstrating a solid, unbending adherence to the faith. The fact that the time limit was being waived to some extent for Kateri did not raise any animosity or envy from her companions. Rather, the chapel was decorated by one and all, becoming a lavish stage for the festivities, as the people sought to honor the events —both the feast itself and her reception of Holy Communion — by incorporating all of the traditional symbols of celebration and reverence. Once again pelts, ribbons, feathers, woven tapestries and other Iroquois ornaments were used to make the chapel a vivid and compelling scene. Certainly the Sault members understood that she was being honored in a singular fashion, and they rejoiced for her.

On the morning of Christmas Day, 1677, Kateri Tekakwitha approached the altar and made her first Holy Communion. She advanced shyly, humbly, quite convinced of her unworthiness to receive Christ, but accounts of the event relate that her face wore such an expression of rapture that her companions were transfixed. She was one with Christ, united with him, moving toward her ultimate destiny, which was the final Beatific Vision in heaven. Nothing else mattered for Kateri Tekakwitha, nothing else had value or even significance in her life.

Following the Christmas celebrations, which were joyous and offered the community not only the happiness of seeing Kateri receive the Holy Eucharist, but filled with the tender moments that always accompany that feast in every land of the world, the Indians began their departure for the winter hunting expedition.

This journey into the wilderness, made with the consent and probably the encouragement of the Jesuits, was an extraordinary facet of French mission life among the Native Americans. Where the Spanish maintained control through village settlements within the missions, the French kept looser reins, providing the converts with a sense of their own identity. All of the tribes of the Five Nations maintained their traditions of hunting and gathering in the wilds. Each one had a particular haven in mind when they set out, one chosen over the decades for its ease, beauty and abundance of game. Kateri and the mission Indians packed up their belongings and walked out of the mission, heading to the Adirondack territory, where the deep forests were mantled in snow, and the air was crisp and clean. Eagles soared above, and the bears slept snug in their caves as the warriors led the way to the designated site. It was always chosen for its closeness to a river or a stream, and for its proximity to the forest. Within these deep woods the hunters would search for beaver, ocelot and other animals, seeking pelts and meat. The expedition was always desired to last for four months, and the people usually returned to their homes refreshed and renewed by the solitude, the silence and the sense of companionship that they shared on the trail and in the encampments.

Because this was a time of independence, a looking back to the days of their past, many of the new converts were placed in a position of some spiritual danger. Without the routine of the mission, without the setting, the chapel and the sacraments, there was a chance that some might relapse into the old ways. For this reason the priests of Sault Mission carefully packed liturgical calendars drawn on bark, as well as prayer schedules and other aids in maintaining an active religious community life. These were carried to the encampment, where they were hung in places of dominance after the cabins of logs and bark skins were erected. It is probable that the remains of cabins were on the site when the people arrived. They were rotted and scarred by the winds and the rains but still evident. The men and women worked together to make the site habitable, and then the Woodland Warriors went off into the woods to see what game they could bring back for the hearths.

It was a time of relaxation, even in the cold and the snows. The women had their usual chores, which included treating any animals brought back to the encampment, but the routine was less formal, and the people were able to relax and spend hours in games and in talk. Kateri went to a nearby stream to seek silence and solitude, and she found a small haven, formed by overhanging branches there. Carving a cross in the trunk of a tree, she fashioned a chapel of sorts and spent hours in prayer, especially during the time she knew that the Mass was being celebrated in the mission chapel at Sault. She united herself to this Mass fervently, seeking to accomplish in a truly spiritual sense what she could not manage physically. Back in the camp, she asked constantly for stories about the saints or the chanting of hymns. Most humored her and found their own conversations elevated more than usual. The days thus passed with their own ease and their own charms, and Kateri spent hours in prayer alone.

One event took place, however, that would have a very distinct bearing on her life and even on her appearances after death. While in the camp, Kateri was asleep on her mat, or else kneeling in prayer there, when a warrior returned from a day of hunting. Exhausted, unable to spend the time finding his own wife's mat in the shadowy confines of the cabin, he stretched out on the floor and fell asleep. In the morning, when his wife awoke and could not find him beside her, she started to look for him. She was shocked to see him asleep close to Kateri, who had retired for a short rest. They were not close enough to touch one another, but the man was definitely sleeping in a place he did not belong. The woman, a sincere and good Christian, kept silent about it, but she began to watch her husband and Kateri for other signs of an affair or an involvement. Her alertness paid off when she saw her husband building a canoe. Asked by someone if he needed help, he laughed and said Kateri could help him. That put the seal on the affair as far as the wife was concerned, naturally, but she waited until the group had returned to Sault Mission before lodging a complaint.

The converts reached the Sault in time for Palm Sunday, and Kateri was introduced to the liturgical events of the Holy Week and the Passion. For someone new to Catholicism, particularly someone not traditionally acquainted with Christianity, the Passion Week observances can have a terrible impact. Kateri must have witnessed some sort of liturgical ceremony of the Passion during her time in her village, but what she saw and heard at the Sault Mission reduced her to tears, filled her with a truly profound horror and prompted her to even greater reparations and self-inflicted penances. Here it must be understood that physical punishment was quite instinctive in the Native American community at the time. Hardships, suffering and physical pain were not new to the Indians, who recognized in them the way of growing in strength and in spiritual power. Particularly those who had led evil lives in the past resorted to such penances. Kateri, struck by the agonies of Christ, attempted to follow in the same path, to endure whatever pain she could in order to transform her flesh and to imitate the Savior.

At the same time, however, God had provided yet another torment, in the form of the woman's suspicions on the hunting expedition. When the group had returned to the Sault, this woman approached Father Cholonec and confided in him. He was quite troubled by the woman, whom he knew to be resolute in the faith and sincere. He calmed the woman, advised her not to spread the story, but he did not react in the way Father de Lamberville had responded with the aunt's tale of an incestuous relationship. The priest went instead to Kateri, hoping that she would silence his doubts and his confusion.

Father Cholonec's actions should be judged by the reality of the situation and by the conditioning which he and others had received as a result of being children of their own historical age. To begin with, the presence of Kateri Tekakwitha in the Sault Mission must have disturbed many. She was so amiable, so pious, so resigned to the will of God, so intent upon prayer and sacrifice, that she must have appeared as an alien being, or as something not quite real. Because of human nature, most men and women tend to discount what they see of goodness and holiness, seeking an underlying cause, a slightly distorted view or a motive. The priests and the other Christian Indians must have wondered silently, if not aloud, how such a paragon of virtue had risen among them. Kateri Tekakwitha was so unlike her Iroquois people, so advanced in spirituality and in saintliness, that she must have been frightening. Father Cholonec, who was charged with the well being of the entire mission, must have wondered as well about the displays of holiness which Kateri evidenced, despite her humility and her reserve. This does not mean that he doubted Kateri. He must have had lingering thoughts about the origin of her actions, the reasons why she was so set apart, so distinguished in matters of the soul.

He went to her with the woman's accusations and was greeted with a calm silence as a result. Kateri listened, did not show shock and did not interrupt his recitation with violent protests. Rather, she calmly announced that nothing of the sort had happened or could happen. She was innocent of all such crimes, and God knew that well enough to provide her with his protection. Father

Cholonec, stunned by her acceptance of the accusation and by her calm and resolute announcement that nothing of the sort was possible, let the matter drop. Some of the other converts, however, did hear of it, as the woman accuser was not as discreet as she should have been, and rumors did spread about Kateri.

They were not malicious stories, just the sort of dreadful tidbits and tales that humans spread about one another. Certainly the mission people talked about Kateri often enough, and one or two dropped hints that perhaps what they glimpsed on the surface was not exactly the truth of the matter. It was part of the human game of slander, the terrible way in which men and women hurt one another without delivering a physical blow. Because of the mission schedule and the attitude of the local populace, however, the rumors remained behind closed doors, hidden and never bursting into the public humiliations which Kateri had suffered in the past. If they looked at her with wonder, they said nothing and made no effort to hinder her spiritual growth.

Actually, on Palm Sunday, when Kateri was allowed to receive Holy Communion for the second time, the entire community was edified by the change which came over her during her union with Christ. That afternoon she was also inducted into the Brotherhood or Confraternity of the Holy Family, a rare honor. If the woman with the suspicions felt irritation or anger over the honor, she said and did nothing. Kateri became one of the select group of Christians at the mission, despite her young age and her lowly status as a new convert. The entire community greeted this advance with the usual demonstration of delight and rejoicing.

Perhaps when confronted by the accusation, or during the following hours, Kateri began to understand that her death was fast approaching. She would have embraced such a premonition with indescribable joy, naturally, as she was about to be set free from a world that she despised and loosened from a flesh that she believed to be only a feeble encumbrance. Her reputation and her good name no longer mattered, and she rejoiced in being reviled for something that she did not do. Christ, the Sinless, had been slain as a common criminal by men of evil ambitions. This sort of mental suffering was mild compared to his pains, and she put all thoughts of her reputation aside. The Heavenly Father would make her known in his time, and her name would be glorified when he chose to confound her enemies and to edify the innocent.

Practical, however, even in the midst of her spiritual consolations and her contemplative prayers, Kateri decided never to attend another hunting expedition. When the group set out later, she refused, and she explained to the priests that the expeditions provided physical benefits but brought cruel sufferings to her soul by denying her the sacraments and the Presence of Christ upon the altar.

An accident which took place while she was out gathering wood and felling trees, convinced Kateri that she was in God's hands alone. A rather large tree limb crashed to the ground, striking her on the head. Unconscious for a time, she was revived by her companion and urged to return to the mission. Kateri only smiled and thanked God for saving her life. She was not anxious to remain on the earth, but she realized that she had been spared for penance and expiation.

Now this profound recognition of her role, of her union with God, demonstrates the spiritual maturity of Kateri Tekakwitha. She had been moving steadily through the levels of the mystical life, first being called to the special relationship, then purging herself of all that she felt offensive to God, then seeking the path by which she could serve him. The last level of such a spiritual ascent is union, the embrace, the becoming one with The One. Kateri achieved this level without any great mystical demonstrations or notoriety. She did not float in the air, did not write great volumes of mystical truths. She was a Mohawk Indian, in the wilderness mission, frail and she was scarred and half blind. Kateri was also chosen by God to be his alone, in the realm of the spirit that few human beings understand or even recognize.

The priests saw the signs. They were trained to perceive changes within their converts, to discern the workings of the Holy Spirit upon distinct souls. Even the other men and women of the mission were beginning to respond more and more to her presence and influence. One such woman, named Marie Theresa Tegaigenta, would discover Kateri and would be changed for the rest of her earthly life.

The woman born Tegaigenta to the Oneida nation, had endured a strange life in the wilderness. She had been baptised Marie Theresa and had become a Christian, lapsing at times into the old ways and forgetting the graces which had been showered upon her in the sacrament. In 1675, with her husband, she came finally to La Prairie Mission and from there went on a winter hunting expedition. Her husband and a nephew were with her, and they joined another group of Iroquois, consisting of four men, four women and three children. All of them were on their way to a campsite normally erected along the Ottawa River. It was part of the mission tradition, and the group looked forward to pleasant days and good hunting.

Several miles into the wilderness, however, the group was caught in a terrible blizzard, with winds and storms raging over their heads. The snow fell everywhere, burying the plants and sending the game into hiding. The hunters in the group were able to kill only one animal, which they cooked and ate to keep up their strength. The meat did not last, of course, and within days they were all starving again, with no change in the weather and no sign of survival.

The women stewed the skins which they carried in their packs, hoping to loosen any bits of flesh or nurturing fats from them and making a soup to feed their companions. While the hunters crashed about in the storm, the women gathered tree bark and soaked that as well, trying to make it edible. Others crawled around on the ground looking for tubers, grass and other plants. Nothing could be provided for the cook pots, and even in shelters the fires went out and the chill of the wind and snow ate into their weakened bodies.

Marie Theresa's husband fell ill as a result, and as she stayed to care for him, two of the hunters went on ahead of the group, hoping to find some dead carcass or some cleared field. One returned from this venture alone, and the others dared not look at him because he appeared well fed and rested. It was obvious to one and all that the warrior had slain his companion and had roasted his flesh in order to stave off his own starvation.

Marie Theresa's husband did not recover, and when the group decided to retrace their steps in hopes of reaching the mission before their hunger slew them on the paths, the warrior who had returned alone from the hunt insisted that she abandon her husband and come with them. She refused, staying by his side until he died a few days later, and she mourned him and buried his corpse so that the scavanging birds and the wild animals would not devour his flesh. Then, carrying her sick nephew on her back she trudged along the trail left by the group and caught up with them. A new round of horrors began there, as the warriors looked at a woman member of the group and her two children, obviously intending to murder them and roast them in order to survive. Knowing that Marie Theresa was a Christian, they asked her opinion of the deed, filling her with revulsion and terror. Knowing that if she tried to stop them the men would slay her and her nephew, she kept silent. Inwardly, however, she was sick with grief and begged God's forgiveness for her cowardice and for her refusal to risk all by stopping them. The woman and her children died at the hands of the warriors, and their bodies were served up as food. Marie Theresa was half hysterical by this time, begging God's forgiveness over and over and promising to change her life if she survived this terrible ordeal. She did survive, one of five who managed to find their way to the mission again. There she confessed her sins to the startled and shocked priest, and she made good her word, taking on herself the Christian way of life with generosity and with a steadfastness that kept her secure in the faith.

She moved with the mission to Sault in 1676 and continued her life there, meeting Kateri Tekakwitha in 1678. The young Mohawk maiden asked her which side she should use in the chapel, adding that she felt that she did not have a right to enter, being sinful and unworthy of such a distinct honor. The words struck Marie Theresa in her heart, and she wept and confided the sordid tale of her conversion, the expedition and her efforts to maintain a life of atonement. Kateri, struck by the horrors that the woman had endured, and by her honesty and obvious sincere desire to live a virtuous life, opened up her own heart, and in time the two women became close friends. Kateri was still living in the cabin and still calling Anastasia "Mother," as she had from the first instant that she was welcomed to the Sault. Anastasia, however, was elderly and now unable to work in the fields or the forests. She remained close to Kateri, but both knew that she needed a companion closer to her own age. Kateri and Marie Theresa thus began to accomplish their daily chores together, went to chapel together and encouraged one another over and over to heights of perfection.

The relationship, of course, was quite unequal in a spiritual sense, as Marie Theresa probably had absolutely no idea of the depths of Kateri's holiness or the mystical form which it had assumed. She was a woman who had experienced the world, had married, had been a drunk, had taken part in a grisly episode on the wilderness trail. The faith was a haven for her as a result, and she lived to atone for her own evils and for the evils of her people. Kateri, who had never sinned — a fact that Marie Theresa reported later by stating that the only fault Kateri could manage to call down upon herself was working in the fields on the sabbath — walked the rare and beautiful landscape of a soul in tune with the vibrancies of Divine Love. They blended, however, sometimes falling into the error of excesses in penance, sometimes trying to assume too many self-inflicted punishments, but always seeking God in their lives and existing within the Presence even in the mundane routines of their mission world.

Sometime after meeting Marie Theresa, Kateri was invited in

some fashion to visit Ville Marie, the city of Montreal, where she discovered aspects of the spiritual life that had been instinctive in her and yet never demonstrated visibly. She returned with a new goal, with a new horizon opening before her, the last stage in her spiritual growth and the one which would transport her into the Divine Embrace forever.

Montreal was originally a Huron settlement, called *Hocelaga*, and visited by Jacques Cartier in 1535. This intrepid explorer was welcomed by over one thousand Hurons on the slopes of Mount Royal, and there he made friends with the Huron nation and with its honorable traditions and lore. Eventually the Hurons abandoned the site, moving to Place Royale on the St. Lawrence River, a settlement founded by the great Champlain. *Hocelaga* ceased to exist, reverting to its natural wild and beautiful state until May 6, 1642, when another Frenchman, Paul de Chomedey, called in accounts the *sieur de Maisonnueve*, arrived and started his colonial town there. He called his settlement Ville-Marie, the Town of Mary, and he erected several residences and a chapel, working toward the construction of a hospital and a school as well. The site was given a civic charter by King Louis XIV of France in 1644 and was well on its way to becoming the seat of New France. Chomedey was honored by being appointed the first governor of the town and probably the immediate region.

Encouraged by this development, two saintly women arrived in Ville Marie to found a hospital, the famed Hotel-Dieu, and the local educational systems. The white children were educated in Ville Marie, and a school was established for the Native Americans at the Mission of La Montagne. Kateri Tekakwitha, probably in the company of a priest and other converts, discovered the work of the women who had arrived to dedicate their lives to Christ and to their fellow human beings, and the sight of them sent her soul soaring.

She actually belonged in a religious convent, as a cloister with its routines and carefully structured spiritual exercises, would have provided her with a stable framework for her own mystical experiences. Native American vocations, however, were unheard of, probably never even contemplated, especially by the whites. They would have been hard pressed to consider any Indian maiden intellectual or spiritually inclined enough to assume such a position of leadership and authority. That racial barrier, a product of the times, did not fall for a considerable length of time. Kateri probably never thought about it either. She knew her place, and certainly, what she was experiencing through grace was well beyond anything the average religious monk or sister understood.

She returned to the mission and spoke of the religious life to Marie Theresa. Another Indian woman joined them, and the three hoped to establish a quasi-religious community on Heron Island, where they could wear similar clothes, follow a prayer life and meditate. One of the women went to Father Cholonec, who greeted the idea with laughter, chuckling later when he noted in the mission account that the idea was put to an end. Again, it was the European prejudice at work, as well as the inability of the whites to comprehend such spiritual aspirations as valid in the souls of the Native Americans. Today many members of the various Indian nations have assumed not only religious roles but appointments as prelates throughout the nation. In Kateri's time, however, the wilderness was still prevailing in the minds of the whites, including the missionaries. In truth, a type of religious organization did take root after Kateri's death, with Marie Theresa leading the devout maidens who wanted to live by the example of the Lily of the Mohawks.

In her home, Kateri was experiencing yet another traditional bias, this one instilled in the hearts of her own people. Once again the subject of marriage was brought up to her. Her "sister" and even Anastasia kept urging her to accept a warrior as a husband. They were acting out of concern for her and because the custom of marriage was so ingrained in the Native American heritage. It was fit and just for a woman to want a husband and children, to desire to become a matron leader and to exercise her authority within the community. Certainly the Iroquois had honored their matrons over the centuries, entrusting them with legal and political rights that were quite sophisticated, especially when compared with the lot of most European women.

Kateri's relative began nagging her, complaining that eventually she would have to have a husband to provide for her, hinting that in time the relatives would not be so willing to make room for her in their cabin. The "sister" gave Kateri three days in which to make up her mind, convinced as Kateri's aunts had been in the village, that the woman would come to her senses and accept the inevitable choice. Kateri went to the priest, who felt perhaps that marriage would safeguard her and yet understood that her soul was destined for a different role. He assured her that she was quite free to choose a virginal existence, and if she did, the mission would always come to her aid. Father Cholonec reported that once she heard those words, Kateri's entire appearance changed. She became radiant and calm, and the peace which had entered her soul in that instant radiated outward. He said that she had "entered veritably into the joy of the Lord." That demonstration, that visible display of union, made the missionary even more cautious about protecting her unusual status. When Anastasia came a few days later to complain that Kateri had refused them all, he scolded her and explained that some souls were chosen to perform distinct and unusual acts for the love of God. Anastasia, confronted with another point of view, accepted the priest's words and returned to the cabin to silence the relatives forever. If they clung to their Iroquois traditions inwardly, they said nothing more to Kateri.

Their words would have had little effect anyway, because Kateri had entered into one of the last phases of her earthly life.

Encouraged by Marie Theresa, who had so much to repent, Kateri undertook heavy physical penances, including beatings, branding herself with faggots, wearing an iron waist chain and even trying to sleep on thorns. She continued the practices, including kneeling in the snow and walking barefoot in the dead of winter. The physical exertions and punishments quickly took their toll. Becoming quite ill, Kateri so alarmed her companion that Marie Theresa went to Father Cholonec to explain what they had been doing. He condemned them and made them promise to show some sort of discretion, even as he recognized the traditions of the Native Americans and the piety that compelled Kateri to undertake extreme measures of sacrifice for God. Kateri began to use discretion and soon was able to continue her normal routines.

She prayed, meditated and asked her Heavenly Father for enlightenment, and there is an indication that she visited Ville Marie a second time, perhaps to observe the Sisters there and to properly evaluate their vows. Whatever preparations she made internally, Kateri finally approached Father Cholonec and asked him to allow her to make a vow of perpetual virginity and chastity. She believed that the purity of thought and action performed by all Christians, especially those who had pledged themselves as Spouses of Christ, had enormous appeal to God, and she wanted to accomplish all that she could while she still had time.

Father Cholonec, of course, was astounded. Such a vow was totally unprecedented in the missions, especially among the Native Americans, whose very traditions ran contrary to such ideals. The missionary understood, of course, that it was astounding that Kateri had held herself aloof from the customary physical activities of the villages, had guarded her virginity and her soul always. Seeing the Sisters in Ville Marie had only confirmed that grace and her instincts had taught her over the years, and she understood now that she was able to pledge herself to Christ for the brief period that she had left. This union, this marriage in the spirit would only be a foretaste of what she would experience when her life ended on the earth. She wanted to be the spouse of the Divine Bridegroom, and she knew that it was a tradition in the Church that pious women were able to take such a pledge upon themselves.

Father Cholonec agreed. Some accounts place doubts as to whether or not he did give his consent, but in his own words he made mention of such a vow. On the Feast of the Annunciation, when the Virgin Mother of God asked the Angel of the Lord how she could become a mother, not having known a man, Kateri Tekakwitha, a daughter of the American wilderness, consecrated her virginity, her purity, and her very soul to Christ. She made this vow on March 25, 1679.

In looking back on the occasion and on the important spiritual step taken by Kateri, Father Cholonec stated that she had never been untrained in virtue. She had been God's servant since the first inklings of faith had made their way into her soul unbidden, even in the uproar and the barbarism of the Mohawk village life. The priests and her fellow Christians taught her the niceties, the rituals and the forms of Christianity, but the Holy Spirit instructed her in the essence, in the profound realities of such beliefs.

In this aspect, Kateri's role in American history becomes ever more defined. Many religious, sincere and faithful, work toward contemplation, toward that "joyful gaze of the soul upon God," but it is not something that can be earned. The mystical grace, the sense and compelling force of unity with the Divine comes unrequested, unsought. God chooses his mystics, his contemplatives, his enraptured souls. He moves in them, he guides and molds and opens the spirit toward the final embrace, which is the consuming fire that some great saints have described in the past. No one can ignite that fire personally, no one can carry a torch into the landscape of the mystic. The fire, the consuming raptures, are God's gifts and the result of grace in a uniquely ordained manner. The fact is that Almighty God chose Kateri Tekakwitha, as he chose St. Rose of Lima in the southern hemisphere. Kateri was not aware of a major role in the history of the Native Americans, although she had a predisposition to understanding that her life would not end in the grave; not in the usual sense of hoping for salvation, resurrection and life everlasting but in the manner of continuing as God's

Servant in the world even when her life's breath had faded. She was like an eagle flying directly into the sun, being consumed, being blinded and still flying, soaring and making her way toward the Uncreated Light.

Kateri began to demonstrate clear signs of what the Church calls the "unitive" way at this stage of her short life. She knelt motionless, totally immersed in prayer in the chapel or in the snow beside the giant cross on the riverbank. She was in communion with God wherever her routine took her, and her rapture was evident on her face. The Native Americans who lived among her noticed the changes as well, and they always said that "Kateri was either at home or in church." She was among them, but her soul was already transfixed, altered by Divine Love. The truly holy in the world display this sort of mystical communion in the way they walk, in the way they talk, and in the way that they greet all things as part of the Divine Plan for mankind. Physical punishments and acts of sacrifice no longer mattered. She had broken free of her own flesh and had blended into the realms of the purified.

Such an individual confounds the world, especially if she is raised up by God in the wilderness, in an age that does not afford her or her people the sort of consideration that they are due. The four landscapes of her existence had blended to form a perfect human, a whole being who was able to offer God praise, thanksgiving and atonement. She was prepared for her death, as she was prepared to work as God's servant beyond the grave.

By the time the winter snows were mantling the earth in early 1680, Kateri Tekakwitha was failing in health, wracked by pain and too weak to carry on her normal duties. She remained in her cabin, unable to attend the services in the chapel and yet filled with calm and with joy. Father Cholonec took to visiting her there, bringing holy pictures that she would hold and study. He also brought writings from the Old and New Testaments, inscribed on birchbark. Kateri spent long hours with these pictures and writings, content to remain in her confined area and yet managing somehow to influence life around her at the same time. The Indians began to visit her as well, asking for her counsel and guidance. They knew that the Lily of the Mohawks was about to leave Sault Mission, soaring away from them in the rapture of love.

Intense physical suffering began soon after her initial collapse. All of the punishments which she had inflicted upon herself took their toll, and her generally frail condition was unable to withstand this last assault. She was unable to move, remaining still on her pallet but demonstrating her serene and gentle outlook. Her condition worsened steadily, and with the approach of Holy Week everyone in Sault Mission recognized the signs of her coming death.

The priests decided to bring her the Viaticum, the communion offered to the sick and the dying. This was an unusual decision, as the priests normally did not carry the Blessed Sacrament out of the chapel in these times. In the early mission stages it was considered too dangerous to expose the Host to the rough and tumble atmosphere of the cabins and the general camps. In Kateri's state, however, it was deemed a necessity. She could not be brought to the chapel on a stretcher, as it was feared that she would not make the short trip alive. No one wanted to deny her the Blessed Sacrament. After consulting with the elders of the mission, the priests informed her that they would bring communion to her in her bed.

Kateri, delighted that such a blessing was going to be given to her, confided in Marie Theresa that she had nothing to wear for the occasion. Although she had made clothing, even elaborate moccasins for everyone else, she had nothing but a ragged shift for her own body. Marie Therese brought a fine outfit for her to wear, and a radiant Kateri awaited the priests who came in a procession with the Blessed Host.

Following her reception of the Holy Eucharist, Kateri was visited by all of her mission companions. The Brotherhood of the Holy Family especially remained ever at her side, coming two by two to keep vigil and to see to her comfort. During one of their hours of care, a young woman who had great devotion to Kateri went into the forest to perform harsh physical penances in order to insure an easy death for the Lily of the Mohawks. Kateri knew that she had set out to do this and sent for her. When the startled young woman appeared, Kateri urged her to practice moderation and to be assured that after her death she would pray for her and be a guardian always. The girl was reduced to tears and knelt beside Kateri, remaining at her side.

Her condition worsened steadily, and the others watched as her skin darkened and her body contorted with pain. Father Cholonec, ever watchful, informed her then that he would bring Extreme Unction, the last rites which would put the seal of her faith on her dying body. Kateri told him not to hurry, as she would be able to receive it the next day. She knew the hour of her death and waited with calm for the approaching last embrace. When the priests did return the next day, Kateri was there, watching them with half blind eyes, small, delicate and wrapped in her last mortal agonies. She died soon after the ritual, reciting the names "Jesus" and "Mary." On April 17, 1680, at the age of 24, Kateri Tekakwitha left behind all of the landscapes of this world to begin her true existence in heaven.

The Indians crowded into the cabin to be present at her death, and they wept and mourned their loss. For more than an hour the cabin was filled with the sounds of hearts breaking, but then Father Cholonec and the others discovered the first sign of Kateri in her unearthly vocation.

The body of Kateri had been laid out on a pallet, but it was no longer the frail, dark and scarred young woman that had just expired. Her skin lightened, becoming radiant and white, and the scars vanished from her face, showing the beautiful bone lines and the lovely angles of her heritage. The people gasped, for before them lay an exquisite creature restored. At that point, two Frenchmen who were well acquainted with the Lily of the Mohawks chanced by and entered the cabin. They took one look at the body and asked what lovely maiden slept there, surrounded by the people. Father Cholonec explained that it was Kateri, who had died just an hour before, and the two Frenchmen knelt beside her and wept. They were stunned by the changes, which they knew demonstrated Kateri's true beauty in the eyes of God. They volunteered to make an elaborate coffin for her burial and set out to take down the trees and begin carving the box that would hold her remains.

The coffin and the rituals of the funeral were chosen especially for Kateri, as the Native Americans even in the mission kept to their traditional burial rites normally. With their sense of oneness with the earth, the Indians did not go to great lengths to protect the body from natural decay. Most were wrapped in blankets or in some other prepared shroud and placed gently in the earth, where the months would reduce the flesh and the bone to the elements of the soil. Kateri, however, was to be placed in a coffin and buried beside the great cross on the riverbank, where all could visit her gravesite. She had once been asked by the priests about her choice of burial, and she had said that she would like to be placed near the cross, beside the lovely river, with Heron Island in the distance and the sounds of nature echoing over her head. The wind blowing through the forests, the cry of the loon, the sound of distant geese wending their way in formations across the horizon would resound there, reflecting the nurturing of the earth and the endless abundance offered to mankind by Almighty God. She was interred there, with all of the mission population in attendance, some quite inconsolate. The woman, for example, who had accused Kateri of evil during the winter hunting expedition, had to be restrained from doing genuine violence to herself after Kateri died. As the Lily of the Mohawks had understood, God was the true keeper of her honor and her reputation.

Word of her death swept beyond the mission compound, of course, carried by the two awed Frenchmen and by others. The phrase was always the same when relaying the sad tale: "The saint is dead." No one needed to hear the name, as those words carried enough detail. As she had been called "the Christian" in her Mohawk village, so she was called "the Saint" at Sault. Other Indians and whites from Ville Marie and elsewhere began arriving unbidden at the mission as soon as the word spread, and the priests watched as hundreds knelt before the grave and prayed or wept. Within a few months, in fact, Kateri was being called "the Protectoress of Canada" among the faithful. In 1688, Bishop de St. Vallier, who had visited the Sault and had been so edified by the Christian community there, stated:

> Here at the Sault, one may see, in the person of Kateri Tekakwitha, the first Christian Virgin which the Iroquois nation has given to the Church of Jesus Christ. God has permitted many wonders to take place at the tomb of this marvelous girl.

The wonders were taking place. The sick and the lame were being brought to her grave, where they were healed. In time small packets of dirt from her grave were used as well, curing people throughout the territory. Novenas and prayers, the touch of one of her moccasins or crosses, the thought of Kateri was all that was necessary for other human beings to be relieved of their physical sufferings. She was performing as the Servant of God, as she had promised. For some, however, Kateri involved herself even more fully.

Father Chauchetiere was the first one to see Kateri after her funeral. Six days after she was buried beside the cross on the river bank, he was working in the church and looked up to see her standing beside him. Radiant, smiling and emanating pure joy, she was accompanied by two other images: a church turned upside down and a Native American tied to a flaming stake. The priest, shocked and shaken, watched in silence for several hours, trying to understand what Kateri was telling him. Three years later, he and everyone else knew her message, as it was carried out by two rather terrible events. A tornado struck the village during one frightful storm, and the church was lifted from the ground, swirled in the air and then set on the earth again, upside down. Three priests were inside the church when it was lifted by the storm, and when the structure fell to the ground and shattered, they were discovered bruised but generally unharmed. The second image had foretold a more terrible event, which came about when the Onondagas attacked the mission during a period of inter-tribal warfare. An Iroquois Christian was taken captive, and the Onondagas burned him alive. They reported later that the man died in agony, not cursing them or wailing to be set free. Even in his last torments he exhorted them to accept Christ and to take on the freedom, the wholeness, the beauty of the faith in their lives.

Anastasia, the "mother" of Kateri, was the second person to see her after her death. Early one morning, while sleeping, she heard Kateri's voice echoing beside her bed. "Mother," the young woman called, "open your eyes and look at me." When she did manage to look at the vision, Anastasia saw a radiant and lovely Kateri standing before her, holding a shining cross. Kateri said that she had loved the cross while on earth and loved it even more in paradise.

Marie Theresa, who had felt the loss of Kateri perhaps more than anyone else, reported that Kateri appeared to her one day to chide her about a particular fault and to encourage her to redouble her efforts and to look to heaven. Marie Theresa started a group called the Sisters of Kateri, joined by several other young Indian converts. They lived semi-religious lives, maintaining the standards of perfection and purity that Kateri had so exemplified in her lifetime.

Father Chauchetiere, however, was to be visited yet again. He found himself in the company of Kateri a second time, and during this vision she asked him to paint her portrait and to provide other pictures to inspire her people to accept the Catholic faith. He was troubled by the vision, naturally, and he started the portrait, stopped and then began again. Apparently it was a rather strange picture when completed, as Father Cholonec referred to it in the records as "somewhat original." That portrait worked a miracle instantly, and the local populace began to clamor for more. The priest was drawing or painting Kateri everyday. It was evident that other objects had the same healing qualities. Because of the overwhelming powers of Kateri to aid the ones she had left behind, she was called the "Thaumaturge," the healer of the New World. The cures were dated by authorities as they happened.

Even Hot Cinders benefited from the young woman that he had aided so many years before. The chief's wife was terribly ill and in danger of dying when Kateri's coverlet was brought to her bed. Wrapped in the coverlet, she was cured instantly.

In time, of course, as the frontiers changed and the tensions of the wilderness rose, Mission Sault had to be moved. The people took down their cabins, their stockades and their chapel complexes, packing them up for the trek to a new site. Kateri's coffin was dug out of the ground and carried with the other precious items from the chapel and the mission proper. Her remains were reburied in each new mission site, because the people would not part with her, would not allow the enemies of the faith to despoil them forever. In time, her relics, parts of her remains, were distributed to other Native American mission outposts. A monument was also erected in her memory at Auriesville, New York, where it serves today as a symbol of her life and her enduring service over the centuries. The monument reads:

Catherine Tekakwitha
April 17, 1680
The Most Beautiful Flower That
Ever Bloomed For The Indians.

Her cause was opened soon after her death, as the authorities in Rome were alerted to her miracles, cures and apparitions. Kateri, however, was not given the honors of the altar in the Church until 1942, when she was declared Venerable in Rome. The activities concerning her life and memory, realities which have united the Native Americans of many nations in the faith, continued unabated, growing always as associations and pious groups were formed in reservation areas or in urban sites where the Indian population was strong enough. Miracles were recorded, and cures were documented. The cause advanced steadily, and in June 1980, she was declared Blessed. A vast contingent of Native Americans went to Rome and took part in the celebrations held there, delighting the European spectators who were thrilled by the appearance of the tribes and their regalia.

Everywhere throughout the United States and Canada those who could not attend the ceremonies in Rome held their own festivities. So well known is Kateri, in fact, that a remarkable gathering was conducted in her name in Honolulu, Hawaii. The Hawaii Council of Indian Nations, a unique organization representing more than 3,000 Native American residents of the Hawaiian Islands, from sixty separate nations, invited the islanders to join them in a Mass and reception. Well attended, the festivities allowed the Native Americans to share their culture, their traditions and the honors of America's only Native American Christian mystic.

Such devotion to Kateri did not end with the honors at the altar.

Pious societies and organizations collect word of her ongoing intercessions, taking testimonies and asking for documentation of the miracles that she continues to shower upon the Americas. Among the valued treasures of Kateri's life, including her personal effects which have survived over the centuries and her shrine, are the descendants of Kateri's own family. One outstanding member of Kateri's clan was Chief Henry J. George, who worked tirelessly for her cause until his death in October 1991.

The organizations that are active in the cause and in the spread of Kateri's message to the world, hold annual observances, symposiums, conferences, camps, prayer sessions, Masses and other spiritual activities. Awards are given to those who have honored Kateri in a singular fashion, and word of her life and virtues is spread through the publications of the associations. Some very devoted men and women have given of their time and talents to secure Kateri's place, not only in the Native American environment but in the general American populace as well. Letters received in the organizations come from people of all races and all walks of life, these having benefited from Kateri's unceasing intercessions.

Anyone wishing to learn more about the modern activities and associations honoring Kateri Tekakwitha should contact the following organizations:

Monsignor Paul A. Lenz
Director
Bureau of Catholic Indian Missions
2021 H Street, N.W.
Washington, DC 20006
(the prayer cards are distributed by this office)

Reverend John J. Paret, S.J.
Tekakwitha League
Auriesville, NY 12016

Tekakwitha Conference National Center
P.O. Box 6768
Great Falls, MT 59406.

These organizations publish newsletters, books and other articles and welcome inquiries and reports of Kateri's intercessions. They also welcome aid and support for their continuing efforts, not only to spread the word of Kateri Tekakwitha but to aid the Native Americans, her people.

A prayer for the canonization of Kateri Tekakwitha has also been approved and is being distributed. The prayer reads:

O God, who, among the many marvels of Your Grace in the New World did cause to blossom on the banks of the Mohawk and of the St. Lawrence, the pure and tender Lily, Kateri Tekakwitha, grant we beseech You, the favor we beg through her intercession; that this Young Lover of Jesus and of His Cross may soon be counted among her Saints by Holy Mother Church, and that our hearts may be enkindled with a stronger desire to imitate her innocence and faith. Through the same Christ our Lord. Amen.